Law, Society & Politics

Marvin L. Astrada

Law, Society & Politics

A Critical Analysis of U.S. Supreme Court Power in the Political & Legal Process

palgrave
macmillan

Marvin L. Astrada
New York University
Washington, DC, USA

ISBN 978-3-030-66713-9 ISBN 978-3-030-66714-6 (eBook)
https://doi.org/10.1007/978-3-030-66714-6

This Palgrave Macmillan imprint is published by the registered company Springer Nature Switzerland AG
The registered company address is: Gewerbestrasse 11, 6330 Cham, Switzerland

I dedicate this work to my wife and daughter, who continually inspire me to reflect honestly, critically, and seek authentic explanation and understanding of the complex world we inhabit.

Contents

CHAPTER 1

Step 1: Backgrounder for an Exercise in Disaggregation

Abstract Questions pertaining to the character and content of the "American People" have assumed center stage. What exactly is an American? Who or what comprise the People? What are the constitutive sociocultural, political, and economic ordering principles of the American People and society? Is there, in actuality, an authentic, distinct, and viable national American political identity or community? Or are the cavernous ruptures, fissures, and balkanization that seem to permeate law, society, and politics in the present indicative of a genuine crisis of legitimacy, cohesion, and national community? What is the role of the U.S. Supreme Court in this milieu? How does it impact law and policy? From a sociocultural, economic, political, and ideological perspective, the Court's singular proclamations as to what the Constitution means, its purpose, and how it is to be perceived and implemented have profound consequences for representational politics and notions of what constitutes the American polity.

Keywords US Supreme Court · Elitism · Representation and the people · Democracy · Constitutional law

Since the 2016 U.S. presidential election, the American polity has experienced a variety of intense and persistent challenges characterized by some

M. L. Astrada, *Law, Society & Politics*,
https://doi.org/10.1007/978-3-030-66714-6_1

as constituting, in part, a profound existential, political, and ideological identity crisis.[1] Critical questions pertaining to the character and content of the "American People" have assumed center stage in the realms of law, society, and politics. What exactly is an American? Who or what comprise the People?[2] What are the constitutive sociocultural, political, and economic ordering principles of the American People and society? Is there, in actuality, an authentic, distinct, and viable national American political identity or community? Or are the cavernous ruptures, fissures, and balkanization that seem to permeate law, society, and politics in the present indicative of a genuine crisis of legitimacy, cohesion, and national community?[3]

Is the People an organic, self-contained, self-evident concept that preexists the Constitution? Is the signifier of the People indicative of an independent state of affairs? Or did "'James Madison and his colleagues at

[1] This introductory chapter is drawn from, in part, Marvin L. Astrada, The People: A Pre-Primer for Critically Reevaluating Representation & Court Power in the Present, 88 *Fordham L. Rev.* Online 156 (2020). See E.J. Dionne Jr., et al., The Munk Debates: Is American Democracy in Crisis? (2018).

[2] A common view—one that has weighty implications for public policy—is that the "United States and its constituent States, unlike foreign nations, are 'kindred systems,' 'parts of ONE WHOLE.' They compose one people, bound by an overriding Federal Constitution." *Gamble v. United States*, 139 S. Ct. 1960, 1990 (2019) (citations omitted) (Ginsburg, J., dissenting). The notion of a "whole people" is an enduring notion (irrespective of its truth or validity). The lodestar of the Constitution's genesis, purpose, meaning, and authority is the People. The Court has declared that, "in all six other provisions of the Constitution that mention 'the people,' the term unambiguously refers to all members of the political community, not an unspecified subset." *D.C. v. Heller*, 554 U.S. 570, 580 (2008).

[3] "[G]overnment has nothing to do with social, as distinguished from technically legal, rights of individuals. No government ever has brought, or ever can bring, its people into social intercourse against their wishes. Whether one person will permit or maintain social relations with another is a matter with which government has no concern. I agree that if one citizen chooses not to hold social intercourse with another, he is not and cannot be made amenable to the law for his conduct in that regard; for no legal right of a citizen is violated by the refusal of others to maintain merely social relations with him. What I affirm, however,] is that no State, nor the officers of any State, nor any corporation or individual wielding power under state authority for the public benefit or the public convenience, can, consistently either with the freedom established by the fundamental law, or with that equality of civil rights which now belongs to every citizen, discriminate against freemen or citizens, in those rights, because of their race, or because they once labored under disabilities of slavery imposed upon them as a race." *Civil Rights Cases*, 109 U.S. 3, 59 (1883) (Harlan J., dissenting).

Philadelphia in 1787 [... actually] invent[] the American people?' ... The opening words 'We the People' are among the most quoted and pregnant words in the nearly sacred text of the Constitution."[4] The question of the People, its character and content, its purpose, meaning, and role in structuring American government and the interpretation of the fundamental law, remains as pressing in the present as it did at the founding. This is especially the case since the Court has very forcefully stated that the "constitution was an act of the people of the United States ..."[5]

The American polity has been confronted with a plethora of challenges, recent as well as endemic and continual, such as: the COVID-19 viral pandemic, police brutality and qualified immunity, structural racism, social unrest, national security and foreign relations, impeachment, the environment, government interrelations, the U.S. Capitol riots, and the prominence of identity politics in the 2020 presidential election.[6] Profound events, such as the U.S. War on Terror (2001–present), the U.S. response to the COVID-19 viral pandemic (2020–present), the recent global and domestic protests condemning police killings of marginalized subcommunities, and the occupation of the Capitol by rioters rejecting the results of the 2020 election do not seem to reflect a

[4] Ralph D. Church, We the People: Reflections on the Meaning of the 'People' in the Constitution of the United States of America, *Il Politico*, vol. 57, no. 2 (162) (Aprile-Giugno 1992) 259.

[5] *Martin v. Hunter's Lessee*, 14 U.S. 304, 332 (1816).

[6] See Freedom House, "Democracy in Retreat: Freedom in the World 2019," available https://freedomhouse.org/report/freedom-world/freedom-world-2019/democracy-in-retreat; Simon Tisdall, "American Democracy Is in Crisis, and Not Just Because of Trump," *The Guardian*, August 7, 2018, available https://www.theguardian.com/commentisfree/2018/aug/07/american-democracy-crisis-trump-supreme-court; Julia Azari, "It's the Institutions, Stupid: The Real Roots of America's Political Crisis," *Foreign Affairs*, July/August 2019, available https://www.foreignaffairs.com/articles/united-states/2019-06-11/its-institutions-stupid; Sheryl Gay Stolberg and Nicholas Fandos, "Pelosi Declares Nation Is in a 'Constitutional Crisis,'" *New York Times*, May 9, 2019, available https://www.nytimes.com/2019/05/09/us/politics/pelosi-constitutional-crisis.html; David Kaiser, How Today's American Crisis Is Different, *Time*, July 22, 2016, available https://time.com/4417672/american-crisis-history/; James Frater, et al., "World Leaders Condemn 'Horrifying' Riot at US Capitol Building," CNN, January 7, 2021, available https://www.cnn.com/2021/01/06/world/world-reaction-us-capitol-riot-intl/index.html.

sustained, inclusive national community or mass national communitarian-based responses to crises. Socioeconomic, racial, and ethnic subcommunities, in particular, have been differentially impacted by nationalist-based responses.[7]

What exactly is the role of the U.S. Supreme Court in this milieu? How does it affect and effect the nationalist character and content of the legal process? From a sociocultural, economic, political, and ideological perspective, the Court's singular proclamations as to what the U.S. Constitution means, what is its purpose, and how it is to be perceived and implemented have profound consequences for democratic

[7] The Supreme Court has acknowledged the nebulous, relative, politicized, and plastic nature of race/ethnicity in its jurisprudence. For example, in *Regents of the Univ. of Cal. v. Bakke*, 438 U.S. 265, 295–96 (1978), Justice Powell noted that "the difficulties entailed in varying the level of judicial review according to a perceived 'preferred' status of a particular racial or ethnic minority are intractable. The concepts of 'majority' and 'minority' necessarily reflect temporary arrangements and political judgments. . . . [T]he white 'majority' itself is composed of various minority groups, most of which can lay claim to a history of prior discrimination at the hands of the State and private individuals . . . There is no principled basis for deciding which groups would merit 'heightened judicial solicitude' and which would not." See also *McCleskey v. Kemp*, 481 U.S. 279, 316 n. 39 (1987) ("[I]n our heterogeneous society the lower courts have found the boundaries of race and ethnicity increasingly difficult to determine.") (citations omitted). See also, Jim Zarroli, The Rich Really Are Different. They Can Shelter in Nicer Places, *NPR*, April 15, 2020, available https://www.npr.org/2020/04/15/834247954/the-rich-really-are-different-they-can-shelter-in-nicer-places; Abby Vesoulis, Coronavirus May Disproportionately Hurt the Poor—And That's Bad for Everyone, *Time*, March 11, 2020, available https://time.com/5800930/how-coronavirus-will-hurt-the-poor/; Katya Fels Smyth, COVID-19 and Health (and Death) Disparities, *Forbes*, March 17, 2020, available https://www.forbes.com/sites/katyafelssmyth/2020/03/17/covid-19-and-health-and-death-disparities/#15a7b0307712; Reggie Jackson, The Impact of Racism Is the "Other Coronavirus Crisis" for People of Color, Milwaukee Independent, March 27, 2020, available http://www.milwaukeeindependent.com/featured/reggie-jackson-impact-racism-coronavirus-crisis-people-color/; Helen Regan et al., Black Lives Matter Protests Across the US, CNN, June 9, 2020, available https://www.cnn.com/us/live-news/black-lives-matter-protests-george-floyd-06-09-2020/index.html; Ruth Bender and David Winning, Antiracism Protests Erupt Around the World in Wake of George Floyd Killing, *WSJ*, June 7, 2020, available https://www.wsj.com/articles/protests-over-george-floyd-killing-spread-to-cities-around-the-world-11591524556; Hakeem Jefferson, Fabian G. Neuner and Josh Pasek, Black Americans Support the Floyd Protests. Whites Are Divided. Here's Why, *Washington Post*, June 10, 2020, https://www.washingtonpost.com/politics/2020/06/10/black-americans-support-floyd-protests-whites-are-divided-heres-why/.

representational politics and notions of what exactly constitutes the American polity.[8] From a structural perspective, for instance, Supreme Court Justices and federal judges "hold a prestigious place in our judicial system, and they earn [at least] double the income of the average American household. How does the privileged socioeconomic status of judges affect their decisions on the bench? ... [in] the 'unselfconscious cultural elitism' of judges. This elitism can manifest as implicit socioeconomic bias."[9] President Lincoln's observation in 1861 thus remains quite relevant today as far as assessing the impact and consequence of the Court on democratic politics and representative government:

> I do not forget the position assumed by some that constitutional questions are to be decided by the Supreme Court .... At the same time, the candid citizen must confess that if the policy of the Government upon vital questions affecting the whole people is to be irrevocably fixed by decisions of the Supreme Court, the instant they are made... the people will have ceased to be their own rulers, having... resigned their Government into the hands of that eminent tribunal.[10]

In light of the foregoing questions and observations, this work employs a critical, conceptual, and structural approach to reexamine the Court's power, and its impact on government, governance, politics, law, and society in the present. More specifically, the modus operandi of the Court's power to interpret and give the final word as to what constitutes the fundamental law[11] rests upon a key notion that merits attention and

[8] See, e.g., *Trump v. Hawaii*, 138 S. Ct. 2392, 201 L. Ed. 2d 775 (2018) (Wherein the Court found that the Executive fulfilled requirement, for Immigration and Nationality Act provision delegating authority to President to suspend entry by aliens or classes of aliens, of finding that entry of aliens from covered countries would be detrimental to interests of U.S.).

[9] Michele Benedetto Neitz, Socioeconomic Bias in the Judiciary, 61 *Clev. St. L. Rev.* 137 (2013).

[10] Abraham Lincoln, ABRAHAM LINCOLN, Inaugural Address, March 4, 1861, quoted in John N. Hostetrler and Thomas W. Washburne, The Constitution's Final Interpreter: We the People, 8 *Regent U. L. Rev.* 31 (1997).

[11] "Fundamental law" in this writing refers to interpretation of the U.S Constitution. The Federalist Papers no. 78 (Alexander Hamilton), available https://avalon.law.yale.edu/18th_century/fed78.asp. "A constitution is, in fact, and must be regarded by the judges, as a fundamental law." Id.

critical analysis, i.e., the *People*.[12] The Court has emphatically declared that, "Ours is a 'government of the people, by the people, for the people.'"[13] This work therefore analyzes the signifier of the People as a political, legal, sociocultural, and ideological process and discursive construct, and examines its impact on a purportedly democratic society premised on authentic representational politics.[14] The *People*, as a concept and in application, is subjected to a biaxial analysis: (1) as a construct manufactured for public consumption by the Court in its constitutional jurisprudence, and (2) as a complex sociocultural, economic, and political signifier that encompasses and impacts the *peoples*—the actual physical peoples that constitute the U.S. population.

Given the macroscopic nature of the foregoing questions, which directly inform this work, a structural conceptual approach comprised of (1) a binary framework and (2) a sociocultural law-as-process perspective, is employed to provide a working context in which to frame and examine said questions. It is important to note at the outset that the overarching aim of this work is to engage in a theoretical investigation that is exploratory in nature—one that seeks to raise more questions rather than the provision of definitive answers. Establishing the groundwork for further examination of the sundry concepts, principles, as well as the legal, political, and policy effects analyzed and discussed, is another aim of this work. This work is merited because the modus operandi of the Court's power regarding the administration of justice, broadly conceived, vis-à-vis its interpretation of the fundamental law, is part and parcel connected to and functions within highly contentious and polarized

[12] The "People" as employed in this writing is indicative of an objective signifier that draws on and perpetuates the notion of a homogenous, unitary signified, as presented, e.g., in the initial U.S. Constitution. The "people" is indicative of a subjective signifier that reflects the diversity of the actual people(s) incorporated/excluded in positing the People. See Daniel Chandler, Semiotics: The Basics 14–15 (2d ed. 2007) ("Focusing on linguistic signs (such as words) . . . a sign [is defined] as being composed of a 'signifier' (signifiant) and a 'signified' (signifié). Contemporary commentators tend to describe the signifier as the form that the sign takes and the signified as the concept to which it refers."). An identity signifier, e.g., is comprised of a signifier, e.g., Black, Gay, or Latino, and a signified concept, e.g., Racial, Sexual, or Ethnic identity.

[13] *U.S. Term Limits, Inc. v. Thornton, 514 U.S. 779*, 821 (1995).

[14] As noted by the Court in its discussion of the "Security of a Free State," the "'state' is used in various senses [and in] its most enlarged sense it means the people composing a particular nation or community." *D.C. v. Heller*, 554 U.S. 570, 597 (2008).

sociocultural, economic, and political contexts. Despite this reality, the Court has continued to present itself as an apolitical governmental institution that is able to produce interpretations free of the taint of (explicit) political, ideological, and sociocultural bias. Yet, it is indisputably the case that, "Constitutional law is political. It results from choices about concerns of government that political philosophers ponder, like liberty and property. When the court deals with major issues of social policy, the law it shapes is the most inescapably political."[15]

As will be discussed below, it is very important to note that a structural approach to law, society, and politics assumes that the judiciary and the law do not function in a vacuum. The judiciary and the law are sociocultural, political, ideological, and economic in nature. The judiciary actively produces textual artifacts, i.e., judicial opinions, that are products and producers of truth, knowledge, and power. Manifold nexuses bind the law and the Court to each of the foregoing state of affairs, rendering law itself a deeply complex and interactive systemic state of affairs.[16] In this work, the employment of a binary framework compliments but does control or determine the outcome(s) of a critical analysis of the Court's power or the role of the People in its jurisprudence. As discussed in more detail below, a binary framework, in conjunction with a sociocultural law-as-process perspective, sheds light on the interstices that exist between the intersection of process with basic binaries that permeate law, politics, and society.[17]

The binary and process perspectives are employed to initiate the disaggregation of the various issues and problems that emerge when critically assessing the Court's power to unilaterally and unequivocally declare the fundamental law. Assessing the impact and consequentialness of Court power and its relationship to and impact on democratic politics and society is effectuated via a binary framework and critical sociocultural

[15] Editorial, "Politics and the Court," *New York Times*, February 5, 2011, available https://www.nytimes.com/2011/02/05/opinion/05sat1.html. For a nuanced analysis of judicial politics, see Brian Z. Tamanaha, The Several Meanings of "Politics" In Judicial Politics Studies: Why "Ideological Influence" Is Not "Partisanship," 61 *Emory L. J.* 759 (2012).

[16] See Sheldon Goldman and Thomas P. Jahnige, Eastonian Systems Analysis and Legal Research, 2 *Rutgers-Cam L. J.* 285 (1970).

[17] See M. King and C. Thornhill, Niklas Luhmann's Theory of Politics and Law (2003); Jill Frank, A Democracy of Distinction: Aristotle & the Work of Politics (2005).

process perspective. The desired effect of the proffered analysis is to (1) raise critical questions, (2) situate the Court in the overarching legal, societal, and political system, (3) provide alternative ways of conceptualizing the Court's power, and (4) analyze the impact of Court power on democratic politics and government. The aim is NOT to provide definitive answers to the questions posed at the outset. Nor is it to provide a fully comprehensive analysis of the myriad complexities and contradictions that emanate from the exercise of the Supreme Court's power. Rather, the expansion of perception, thought, potential, and possibilities of explaining, assessing, and understanding the Court's power and impact on the polity informs this work.

MEF: The Utility of Employing a Binary Framework

Granted, binaries, which classify phenomena biaxially, tend to simplify, distort, and are characterized by reductionism. Nonetheless, when conceptualizing human phenomena, binaries find powerful expression in thought and practice, e.g., in law, where one is either Innocent/Guilty in the criminal context or Liable/Not Liable in the civil context.[18] One does not have to subscribe to the rigidity of the static arrangement of terms within a binary when using it to generate explanatory frameworks.[19] The prevalence of the binary in law and society, despite its shortcomings, can be used as a tool to complement critical analysis.[20] This being the case, a Mass-Elite Framework (hereinafter MEF)—with the caveat that binaries are by no means comprehensive and do fail to capture the deep

[18] Such binaries are underpinned by sub-binaries, such as the Reasonable/Unreasonable Person in the criminal law context. For a discussion of the reasonable person, see Marvin L. Astrada and Scott B. Astrada, Law, Continuity & Change: Revisiting the Reasonable Person Within the Demographic, Sociocultural & Political Realities of the 21st Century, 14 *RUTGERS J. L. & PUB. POL'Y* 196 (2017), available http://www.rutgerspolicyjournal.org/sites/jlpp/files/Astrada.pdf.

[19] See generally Julie A. Greenberg, Deconstructing Binary Race and Sex Categories: A Comparison of the Multiracial and Transgendered Experience, 39 *SAN DIEGO L. REV.* 917, 942 (2002) (discussing how the binaries present in race classifications systems can provide solutions for the current gender binaries).

[20] See Marvin L. Astrada and Scott B. Astrada, Reexamining the Integrity of the Binary: Politics, Identity, and Law, 17 *U. Md. L.J. Race Relig. Gender & Class* 173 (2017), available https://digitalcommons.law.umaryland.edu/rrgc/vol17/iss2/2/.

complexity of human affairs[21]—is employed in this work. MEF provides a conceptual framework in which to contextualize, explain, and begin to understand the basic background in which the political and legal process are situated, and how each impacts and is impacted by the exercise of the Court's power.[22] MEF classifies sociocultural, economic, and political states of affairs as being basically divided into a mass v. elites binary. MEF is not the sole determinant or rather structure of power in societal arrangements. It is, however, a prominent one that underpins the American constitutional order.[23] MEF is expressed in preexisting basic binaries that undergird the establishment and perpetuation of those that exercise power, such as Ruler/Ruled, Innocent/Guilty, Controlled/Controller, White/Non-White, and Reasonable/Unreasonable. MEF thus helps illuminate the socioeconomic, -cultural, and -political underpinnings of constitutional discourse. MEF captures the discrete categories of Mass (signifying the actual peoples that constitute the populace) and the Elite (signifying the select with the power and privilege to rule over and in the

[21] Id. See also Greenberg, supra note 20; Elena Loizidou, Judith Butler: Ethics, Law & Politics (2007).

[22] See Neitz, supra note 9 at 137; Susan P. Robbins, From the Editor—The Red Pill or the Blue Pill? Transcending Binary Thinking, 51 *J. of Social Work Education* 1–4 (2015).

[23] See Lawrence Baum and Neal Devins, Why the Supreme Court Cares About Elites, Not the American People (2010). Faculty Publications. 1116, available https://scholarship.law.wm.edu/facpubs/1116; P.J. Charles, History in Law, Mythmaking, and Constitutional Legitimacy, 63 *Clev. St. L. Rev.* 23 (2014–2015); Charles Beard, An Economic Interpretation of the Constitution (1913); Robert E. Brown, Charles Beard and the Constitution: A Critical Analysis (1956).

name of the peoples).[24] MEF locates power, generally or rather structurally speaking, within a conceptual framework in which those that Have and those that Have Not as far as possessing a preponderance of power in substantially shaping the legal, political, and policy process.

The Mass component of MEF can be conceptualized as encapsulating, representing the actual *peoples* as opposed to the Elite component which encompasses and is expressed in the notion of *People*, a formal (corporate) construct through which the peoples are interpreted and given a "voice" by elites in the realms of law, politics and policy. The People functions, in part, as a fulcrum for, and bestows the imprimatur of legitimacy upon, the exercise of Court power. In conjunction with law, the notion of the American *People* undergirds and comprehensively informs the legal and political process, and notions of representative politics and democratic government. The People, from the founding of the American Nation-State through its present iteration, has been utilized as a singular source for legitimizing the authority for elites to rule in the name of and for

[24] See Astrada, "Binary" supra note 21 at 195. In constitutional discourse, the binary, generally and specifically, has found powerful expression, impacting the fabric of American political culture. One of the most famous footnotes in United States Supreme Court jurisprudence, i.e., Footnote Four from *US v. Carolene Products*, captures the entrenchment of the binary. It is, in Justice Powell's words, "the most celebrated footnote in constitutional law." Lewis F. Powell, Jr., "Carolene Products" Revisited, 82 *COLUM. L. REV*. 1087, 1087 (1982). Although Footnote Four did not give rise to the binary nor mark the prominent moment when the Court embedded a binary framework into its jurisprudence, it does mark a very clear moment in time when the binary is explicitly articulated as being an integral part of the genesis of modern equal protection jurisprudence and clarifies the juridical subject in the context of Court interpretation. The Court ponders, in Footnote Four, "whether prejudice against discrete and insular minorities may be a special condition, which tends seriously to curtail the operation of those political processes ordinarily to be relied upon to protect minorities, and which may call for a correspondingly more searching judicial inquiry." Footnote Four becomes the self-referential basis upon which, among other things, the Court has based its tiered scrutiny framework, and adjudges the manner in which a right translates into a constitutional protection. Id. See also *Nixon v. Condon*, 286 U.S. 73, 89 (1932) and *Nixon v. Herndon*, 273 U.S. 536, 541 (1926) (using the Black/White binary to find that a party cannot exclude blacks from voting in its primary); *Pierce v. Soc'y of Sisters*, 268 U.S. 510, 534 (1925) (Private/Public binary to hold that states cannot require children to attend public, rather than parochial, schools); *Meyer v. Nebraska*, 262 U.S. 390, 401 (1923) (relying on a Citizen Nationalist/Alien Foreigner binary to find that states cannot forbid the teaching of a foreign language).

the People.[25] Elite, at the most basic level of analysis, can be defined "as individuals and small, relatively cohesive, and stable groups with disproportionate power to affect national and supranational political outcomes on a continuing basis."[26] The Mass component of the MEF highlights the fact that the mass (peoples) does not, as is the case for elites, exercise "the ability to define phenomena, and secondly the ability to make these phenomena act in a desired manner."[27]

While it the case that the term elite and elitism have "no agreed meaning inside or outside social science,"[28] nonetheless, each provides a degree of insight into the nature and consequentialness of Court power on Constitutional order vis-à-vis representative democratic politics. This is the case because the term elite "draws on a master distinction between elites and non-elites [—the peoples or mass] to advance explanatory constructs."[29] The Court, as an institution, and the Justices, jointly

[25] See John Higley, "Elite Theory in Political Sociology" (2008), available http://citeseerx.ist.psu.edu/viewdoc/download?doi=10.1.1.462.5495&rep=rep1&type=pdf. "Elites may be defined as persons who, by virtue of their strategic locations in large or otherwise pivotal organizations and movements, are able to affect political outcomes regularly and substantially ... They consist not only of prestigious and 'established' leaders – [e.g.,] top politicians, important businessmen, high-level civil servants, senior military officers – but also, in varying degrees in different societies, relatively transitory and less individually known leaders of mass organizations such as trade unions, important voluntary associations, and politically consequential mass movements. 'Counter-elites' are subsumed by this definition because they clearly have the organized capacity, although perhaps mainly through negation, to affect political outcomes regularly and substantially. It is important to stress that this is a limited and specifically political definition of elites. It is restricted to persons who are at the top of the pyramid or pyramids of political, economic, and social power. [One may also] consider all those in a society who enjoy high occupational, educational, or cultural statuses to be elites in a political sense." Id. See also J. Roland Pennock, Democratic Political Theory (1979); Dennis Frank Thompson, John Stuart Mill and Representative Government (1976); Hanna Pitkin, The Concept of Representation (1972); The Federalist Papers, The Avalon Project, Yale University, available https://avalon.law.yale.edu/subject_menus/fed.asp.

[26] Heinrich Best and John Higley, eds., Intro. in The Palgrave Handbook of Political Elites (2018) 3.

[27] Huey P. Newton, The Huey P. Newton Reader, eds. David Hilliard and Donald Weise (2002) 227.

[28] John Higley, "Continuities and Discontinuities in Elite Theory," in Heinrich Best and John Higley, eds., Intro. to The Palgrave Handbook of Political Elites (2018) 29.

[29] Id. at 33.

and severally, meet the criteria for contemporary "conceptions of political elites ... as networks of individuals and small, relatively cohesive, and stable groups with major decisional power."[30] MEF's utility, for the purposes of this examination, is not that elites are or should be viewed monolithically, or that the latter notion should be held in contempt or viewed negatively in and of itself. Elites and elitism are analyzed as to the substantive impact each has on the interpretation and operationalization of genuine democratic representation of the peoples. While distinct from the peoples (or mass), it is the case that

> Elites are differentiated and stratified. Elite differentiation accords primarily with government, economic, military, and other functional sectors in a society. Power distributions and relations among individuals and groups heading these sectors change gradually over time as sectors wax or wane in functional importance. Abrupt and profound crises may also alter elite differentiation. Elite stratification involves 'elites within Elites' variously labeled executive cores, inner leaderships, central circles, and the like.[31]

MEF thus provides insight into the politicized character, content, and dynamics that inform the legal process vis-à-vis interpretation of the fundamental law. How the peoples are expressed, given voice, agency, weight, in the legal and political process are directly affected and effected by how the Court interprets and articulates "We the People" regarding the character and content of federal and State powers. "Consistent with recognizing that elites are central political actors in all hierarchically structured societies, elitism most usefully means identifying and promoting conditions that enhance elite effectiveness. For example, empowering elites, or believing they should be empowered, to act with relative autonomy, lest mass pressures force disastrous policies and undertakings, is elitism."[32] The People, as an ideational construct, and its application in interpreting the Constitutional text, can be viewed as a mechanism, instrument, whereby the power of the Court is enhanced, preserved, reified and perpetuated. The People has the effect of impacting the peoples by way of the Court's control over the degree of legibility

[30] Jan Pakulski, "The Development of Elite Theory," in Heinrich Best and John Higley, eds., Intro. to The Palgrave Handbook of Political Elites (2018) 12.

[31] Higley, "Continuities," supra note 29 at 27.

[32] Id. at 30.

and intelligibility that the peoples exercise, independently of the Court, within the legal process and on the constitutional landscape. The People contributes, in part, to the peoples being "governed by laws made neither by themselves, nor by an authority derived from them."[33]

Elites, generally speaking, can be readily distinguished from the mass or peoples.[34] An elite/mass distinction, in the context of this examination, is based on the degree of direct substantive—as opposed to nominal—participation of the mass, i.e., the peoples, in the legal, political, and policy process, generally speaking. Very high degrees of direct substantive participation and nominal participation in the legal, political, and policy process characterize elites and mass, respectively. Thus, MEF provides a working context to ascertain how elites affect and effect the interpretation of the fundamental law, which is left to the Court—the most insulated institution from public oversight and control. The interpretive enterprise is directly impacted by the Court's highly selective, nonrepresentative, nondemocratic, publicly unaccountable, and life-tenured position in the overarching sociopolitical, legal, and economic order.

While it may be the case that "a direct form of democracy is impossible in any large bureaucratic organization, let alone in a large, complex, and bureaucratically structured nation-state,"[35] this state of affairs does not foreclose the substantive participation and representation of the peoples or mass in the legal process and in policy spaces. The elite filters through which the people's voice are converted and made into a politically, legally, legitimate and viable medium do not necessarily have to foreclose mass input into the constitutional interpretive enterprise. MEF thus provides explanatory insight into how the Court's utilization of the People affects and effects representative democratic politics—irrespective of the founders' intent to institute republican government as a check on the passion and collective power of the people or mass.

[33] *Lee v. Weisman*, 505 U.S. 577, 608 (1992).

[34] "Max Weber diagnosed the deleterious political consequences of plebiscitary democracy, leaderless democracy, and radical popular mobilizations. He viewed charismatic legitimacy and firm electoral mandates as essential insulations of elites from mass pressures. Schumpeter stipulated in his competitive theory of democracy that during periods between elections, elites must be relatively free of mass pressures in order to formulate and implement effective policies." Higley, "Continuities," supra note 29 at 36.

[35] András Korosenyi, "Political Elites and Democracy," in Heinrich Best and John Higley, eds., Intro. to The Palgrave Handbook of Political Elites (2018) 41.

The People is a politicized ideological construct comprised of complex sociocultural, political, and economic norms, values, and power dynamics.[36] Although it is employed in an objective, matter of fact manner in master narratives and discourse, e.g., the People have "spoken" via the vote,[37] the People is an ideological and discursive signifier, a product of relations of power.[38] It is significant that the People is a singular notion that elites rely upon to justify public authority, government, and governance.[39] On its face, the People seems a straightforward signifier. The Preamble "declares who is enacting this Constitution—the people of 'the United States.' The document is the collective enactment of all U.S. citizens. The Constitution is 'owned' . . . by the people, not by the government or any branch thereof. We the People are the stewards of the U.S. Constitution and remain ultimately responsible for its continued existence and its faithful interpretation."[40]

[36] See Marvin L Astrada, Visions of the Republic Symposium: The People: A Pre-Primer for Critically Reevaluating Representation & Court Power in the Present, 88 *Fordham L. Rev.* Online 156 (2019), available https://ir.lawnet.fordham.edu/flro/vol88/iss1/13.

[37] See, e.g., Meg Wagner, et al., "Joe Biden Elected President," CNN, November 8, 2020, available https://www.cnn.com/politics/live-news/trump-biden-election-results-11-07-20/h_7d24d64536fe14b2584de1539302d7c4; Tom Hals and Makini Brice, "'The People Have Spoken': Judges Reject Two More U.S. Election Challenges," Reuters, December 7, 2020, available https://www.reuters.com/article/usa-election-lawsuit/the-people-have-spoken-judges-reject-two-more-u-s-election-challenges-idUSKBN28H20U.

[38] See Michel Foucault, The Essential Foucault: Selections From Essential Works of Foucault, 1954–1984, ed. Paul Rainbow and Nikolas Rose (1994).

[39] See Thomas R. Dye, Top-Down Policymaking (2001).

[40] Erwin Chemerinsky and Michael Stokes Paulsen, Common Interpretation: The Preamble, NAT'L CONST. CTR.: INTERACTIVE CONST., https://constitutioncenter.org/interactive-constitution/interpretation/preamble-ic/interps/37 (emphasis omitted). See also Morris D. Forkosch, Who are the "People" in the Preamble to the Constitution? 19 *CASE W. RES. L. REV*. 644, 649 (1968). "[i]n the Preamble and in the Constitution itself, . . . the term 'people' is found only twice, plus seven times in the amendments; in the Constitution there is no significant current use of 'person' (although five pre-amendment uses may be referred to), while in the amendments proper there is a maximum use of only six such instances; and, finally, in the entirety of the Preamble, Constitution, and amendments, the maximum use of 'people' and 'persons' is therefore found in 15 instances. For a 'government of the people, by the people, for the people,' it seems almost sacrilegious that our fundamental document contains this term only twice, and only nine times if the subsequent amendments are added; and even if 'persons' is thrown in, the significant total rises only to a maximum of 15." Id.

The People, however, is a functional term of art employed by elites to wield legitimate political authority to exercise power in a democratic political system.[41]

> The "Framers envisioned a uniform national system, rejecting the notion that the Nation was a collection of States, and instead creating a direct link between the National Government and the people of the United States. See, e.g., *FERC v. Mississippi*, 456 U.S. 742, 791, 102 S.Ct. 2126, 2154, 72 L.Ed.2d 532 (1982) (O'Connor, J., concurring in judgment in part and dissenting in part) ("The Constitution ... permitt[ed] direct contact between the National Government and the individual citizen"). *U.S. Term Limits, Inc. v. Thornton*, 514 U.S. 779, 803 (1995). In that National Government, representatives owe primary allegiance not to the people of a State, but to the people of the Nation. As Justice Story observed, each Member of Congress is "an officer of the union, deriving his powers and qualifications from the constitution, and neither created by, dependent upon, nor controllable by, the states.... Those officers owe their existence and functions to the united voice of the whole, not of a portion, of the people." 1 Story § 627."[42]

The foregoing encompasses a People's approach to law and its interpretation, which is firmly situated in the elite sectors of government and society, to include the judiciary. The Court has adhered to the ordering principle that the "whole people of America, [are] as one united body."[43] In doing so, the Court has perpetuated an elitist (reductionist) notion of the populace, divesting the diversity, complexity, tensions, and conflicts of the peoples by converting the latter into the People. The People, comprised of a homogenous, unitary notion of the populace, eclipses the peoples as the locus of public interest and the general welfare.[44] While the

[41] See *U.S. v. Verdugo-Urquidez*, 494 U.S. 259, 265 (1990) ("'[T]he people' seems to have been a term of art employed in select parts of the Constitution."). See also *Jacobson v. Massachusetts*, 197 U.S. 11, 22 (1905) ("Although that preamble indicates the general purposes for which the people ordained and established the Constitution, it has never been regarded as the source of any substantive power conferred on the government of the United States, or on any of its departments").

[42] *U.S. Term Limits, Inc. v. Thornton*, 514 U.S. 779, 803 (1995).

[43] *Penhallow v. Doane's Adm'rs*, 3 U.S. 54, 76 (1795).

[44] "[I]t became necessary for the people or colonies to coalesce and act in concert, in order to divert, or break, the violence of the gathering storm; they accordingly grew into *union, and formed one great political body, of which Congress was the directing principle*

Court is clear that the peoples are separate from the States, it concomitantly implies that this is not the case for the national government. The national government, of which the Court is a constituent component, does not make the same distinction, but rather imbricates the peoples into the national government via the People. "[I]t is well settled that the whole people of the United States asserted their political identity and unity of purpose when they created the federal system."[45] The Court, however, has directly contradicted the foregoing in its jurisprudence. In *Carter v. Jury Commn. of Greene County*, wherein the Court held that the an Alabama law "requiring jury commissioners to select for jury service those persons who are generally reputed to be honest and intelligent and esteemed in community for their integrity, good character and sound judgment is not invalid on its face on ground that it leaves commissioners free to give effect to their belief that Negroes are generally inferior to white people and less likely to measure up to statutory requirements," and that "discriminatory exclusion was not shown by mere fact that for many years jury commission had been composed entirely of white men, nor did absence of Negroes from commission compel and order to appoint Negro commissioners."[46]

Conversely, the *peoples*, i.e., a signifier that designates the actual physical subject populations that serve as the initial basis for notions of the People, reflects the Mass component of MEF, and is conceptually distinct from the People. This distinction is a fundamental one. This work expounds upon this difference by exploring the contention that the *peoples*—which reflects a distinct constellation of norms of values that inform law and policy—is more conducive to genuine representation of the actual peoples' interests and wellbeing. The *peoples* is an analytic concept that will be examined in order to better explain and understand how norms and values directly affect and effect the character and content of law, policy and justice. The *peoples* constitutes and reflects a constellation of norms and values that more accurately reflects the realities and

and soul. As to war and peace, and their necessary incidents, Congress, by the *unanimous voice of the people, exercised exclusive jurisdiction, and stood, like Jove, amidst the deities of old, paramount, and supreme.*" *Penhallow v. Doane's Adm'rs*, 3 U.S. 54, 81 (1795) (emphasis added).

[45] *U.S. Term Limits, Inc. v. Thornton*, 514 U.S. 779, 838 (1995) (Kennedy, J. concurring).

[46] 396 U.S. 320 (1970).

public policy interests of subject populations. Integrity, dignity, fairness, impartiality, and equity are the values that undergird the *peoples*. Socioeconomic actualities, e.g., the paucity of financial resources and literacy among those that reside in the lower socioeconomic sectors of society that, in turn, directly and negatively affects and effects the exercise of fundamental rights, are made legible and weighed in the legal process.

Identifying, distinguishing, analyzing, and assessing how a *peoples*-based approach impacts the legal, political, and policy process, in thought and practice, is key to critically appraising the degree of actual representation present in policy spaces. A *peoples* view of law and policy reveals how select norms and especially values impact perceptions of rights, and how rights are exercised; which, in turn, informs thought—which directly informs judgments.[47] As Hamilton notes in Federalist no. 78, the Court "has no influence over either the sword or the purse; no direction either of the strength or of the wealth of the society; and can take no active resolution whatever. It may truly be said to have neither force nor will, but merely judgment."[48] Judgments regarding the character and content of law and policy spaces are key to assessing how rights and representation manifest in empirical application. The peoples thus provides insight into the operationalization of specific values that directly affect and effect the nexus betwixt perception, thought, and judgment in law and resultant policy spaces.

Identification and critical analysis of norms and values, while conceptual in nature, are nonetheless merited because each has a direct impact on constructing policy spaces. Norms and values are cultural instrumentations, policy mechanisms, that operationalize the general welfare of society. Norms embody values, and vice versa. Norms encompass standards and principles of conduct, values encompass general ordering concepts and principles; each functions as a template for elites (political and legal) as well as subjects to utilize, and each contributes to the basis upon which societal structures are premised. Norms and values inform societal assumptions of what is right, good, and important for society, legitimizing public policy,[49] e.g., the social values of equal justice under

[47] See Sextus Empiricus, Outlines of Pyrrhonism, trans. R.G. Bury (1990).

[48] The Federalist Papers no. 78 (Alexander Hamilton), available https://avalon.law.yale.edu/18th_century/fed78.asp.

[49] See Peter Railton, Facts, Values, and Norms: Essays Toward a Morality of Consequence (2003).

law and equality of opportunity assume a fundamental role in the administration of justice. It is important to note that different norms and values result in variegated social structures, and how they are operationalized. If, for instance, liberty is privileged over equality in the formulation of policy, societal structures such as the administration of justice will be differentially affected, in that civil liberties will play a more prominent role than civil rights in policy outcomes.

LAPP: The Utility of Employing a Process Perspective

Additionally, a sociocultural Law-as-Process perspective (hereinafter LAPP) complements MEF. LAPP illuminates the structural sociocultural dynamics that inform the constitutional interpretive enterprise. LAPP helps account for the multifarious and complex nature of the legal process, supplementing MEF's illumination of the basic structuration of societal order.[50] In the case of judging and the administration of justice, MEF and LAPP help to explain and understand how socioeconomic and cultural factors directly inform and impact representational politics. A former chief judge of the Ninth Circuit Court of Appeals, for instance, has noted that,

> There's been much talk about diversity on the bench, but there's one kind of diversity that doesn't exist: No truly poor people are appointed as federal judges, or as state judges for that matter. Judges, regardless of race, ethnicity or sex, are selected from the class of people who don't live in trailers or urban ghettos. The everyday problems of people who live in poverty are not close to our hearts and minds because that's not how we and our friends live ... When you glide your BMW into your underground garage or behind an electric gate, you don't need to worry that somebody might attach a tracking device to it while you sleep. But the Constitution doesn't prefer the rich over the poor; the man who parks his car next to his trailer is entitled to the same privacy and peace of mind as the man whose urban fortress is guarded by the Bel Air Patrol. The panel's breezy

[50] "Among the constant facts and tendencies that are to be found in all political organisms, one is so obvious that it is apparent to the most casual eye. In all societies ... two classes of people appear[—]a class that rules and a class that is ruled. The first class, always the less numerous, performs all political functions, monopolizes power and enjoys the advantages that power brings, whereas the second, the more numerous class, is directed and controlled by the first." Gaetano Mosca, The Ruling Class, Hannah D. Kahn, ed. & trans. (1939) 50.

opinion is troubling on a number of grounds, not least among them its unselfconscious cultural elitism.[51]

The variables of "unselfconscious cultural elitism" and a socioeconomically nonrepresentative bench are exemplars of how elitism (MEF) and socioeconomic sector (LAPP) directly inform the legal, political, and policy process. MEF and LAPP highlight how the immurement of individuals within discursive modalities that "think" the subject, which produce rather than are the product of the subject, occurs when critical appraisal is not conducted from without the rules of formation propagated by elites that control "legitimate" articulations of ordering precepts, such as the People. A MEF lens, in conjunction with LAPP, provides a working and general backdrop in which to examine the Court's power, its place in and impact on constitutional order, and how it gives rise to and impacts the enduring challenges that American democracy and representative politics have had to contend with.[52] LAPP illuminates the structural sociocultural components that inform law. Namely, that the Rule of Law

[51] *United States v. Pineda-Moreno*, 617 F.3d 1120, 1123 (9th Cir. 2010) (Kozinski, J.).

[52] See, e.g., *Obergefell v Hodges*, 135 S. Ct. 2584, 2607–8 (2015) (holding that under the Fourteenth Amendment's Equal Protection Clause and substantive due process the states must provide marriage licenses to same-sex couples and must recognize marriages that were legally licensed and performed in other states); *United States v. Windsor*, 570 U.S. 744, 745 (2013) (holding that the 1996 Defense of Marriage Act is unconstitutional); Lawrence v. Texas, 539 U.S. 558 (2003) (overruling *Bowers v. Hardwick*, 478 U.S. 186 [1986]); *Boy Scouts of America v. Dale*, 530 U.S. 640, 659 (2000) (holding that the constitutional right to freedom of association allowed the Boy Scouts of America (BSA) to exclude a homosexual person from membership in spite of a state law requiring equal treatment of homosexuals in public accommodations); *Romer v. Evans*, 517 U.S. 620, 635 (1996) (striking down Colorado's Amendment 2, which denied gays and lesbians protections against discrimination); *Bowers*, 478 U.S. at 189 (holding that consenting adults do not have a constitutional right to engage in sodomy in private under Due Process Clause); *One, Inc. v. Olesen*, 355 U.S. 371 (1958) (considering the issue of free speech rights with respect to homosexuality); *Plessy v. Ferguson*, 163 U.S. 537, 550–51 (1896) (upholding the constitutionality of racial segregation laws for public facilities as long as the segregated facilities were equal in quality); *The Civil Rights Cases*, 109 U.S. 3 (1883) (holding that the Civil Rights Act of 1875 was unconstitutional because Congress lacked authority to regulate private affairs under the Fourteenth Amendment; also, the Thirteenth Amendment "merely abolishes slavery," and did not necessarily ban race discrimination regarding access to public services); *United States v. Cruikshank*, 92 U.S. 542, 554 (1876) (declaring that the Due Process and Equal Protection Clauses of the Fourteenth Amendment apply only to state action, not to actions by individual citizens).

(hereinafter ROL) can be viewed as a dynamic, complex, and comprehensive state of affairs that informs and is informed by sociocultural, political, and economic factors.[53] The remainder of this chapter will explicate the choice and value of employing MEF and LAPP to examine and evaluate the Supreme Court's power in a democratic society underpinned by a representative political system.

Unearthing the Effects of Elitism in the Administration of Justice: The Utility of a Mass-Elite Framework and Law-as-Process Perspective

How law is conceptualized, defined, and interpreted in the legal and political process has substantial ramifications for the character and content of public policy spaces. In a liberal democratic society, law, the rule of law, and due process are lodestars in safeguarding subjects' civil rights and liberties, and ensuring genuine representation of the subject population's interests in the legal process and administration of justice. Law is the primary mechanism for administering justice in a democratic society. Ideally, law genuinely reflects, represents the real-world interests of its subjects, serving and promoting the wellbeing of those subjects that dwell within its sphere of protections and obligations.[54] Law, in a liberal democratic context, thus seeks to not only order society but also enhance and perpetuate the wellbeing of subjects, premised on the dignity and integrity of the individual, which gives a subject "an intrinsic worth, a value sui generis that is 'above all price and admits of no equivalent.'"[55] Yet, though the latter may encompass the ideals, aspirations, and values that broadly underpin the law, in actuality there are complex power dynamics

[53] See Richard H. Fallon Jr., et al., The Federal Courts and The Federal System 7th ed. (2015); Richard H. Fallon, Jr., Reflections on the Hart and Wechsler Paradigm, 47 *Vanderbilt Law Review* 953 (1994); Myers S. McDougal, "Law as a Process of Decision: A Policy-Oriented Approach to Legal Study" (1956). Natural Law Forum. Paper 6, available http://scholarship.law.nd.edu/nd_naturallaw_forum/6; "The rule of law, evenly applied to minorities as well as majorities, to the poor as well as the rich, is the great mucilage that holds society together." *Papachristou v. City of Jacksonville*, 405 U.S. 156, 171 (1972).

[54] See Immanuel Kant, The Metaphysical Elements of Justice, trans. John Ladd (1965) 33–45.

[55] John Ladd, Introduction in Immanuel Kant, The Metaphysical Elements of Justice (1965) ix.

at work in the interpretive enterprise and administration of justice that supersede the ideals and technical application of the law.

Law also reflects the degree to which complex sociocultural, political, and especially economic variables directly affect and effect the character and content of public policy that is informed or created via law. Law, and the legal process that effectuates policy, is purportedly administered in a logical, fair, and objective manner that reflects the norms and values of society at large. When law and the legal process are critically examined, however, there are variegated states of affairs, e.g., elitism, hierarchy, stratification, socioeconomic sector, worldview, and ideological posture, that affect the administration of justice. There are, therefore, competing constellations of norms and values that undergird notions of justice potentially at odds with the ideals of law that reflects the dignity and integrity of the subject, and that assume a profound role in how justice will manifest empirically.[56]

Elitism is embedded in the DNA of American constitutional history, politics, and the U.S. Constitution, the lodestar of the American nation-state.[57] Elitism is not a novel phenomenon nor alien to American politics and society.[58] It has, however, assumed an explicit, distinctive, and active

[56] See, e.g., Anti-Federalist Papers # 80, which critiques the character and content of Court power: "[The Court] will give the sense of every article of the constitution, that may from time to time come before them. And in their[, i.e., the Justices,] decisions they will not confine themselves to any fixed or established rules, but will determine, according to what appears to them, the reason and spirit of the constitution. The opinions of the supreme court, whatever they may be, will have the force of law; because there is no power provided in the constitution that can correct their errors, or control their adjudications. From this court there is no appeal." Id., available http://resources.utulsa.edu/law/classes/rice/Constitutional/AntiFederalist/80.htm.

[57] See, e.g., The Federalist no. 63 (Alexander Hamilton or James Madison); Steven R. Boyd, Antifederalists and the Acceptance of the Constitution: Pennsylvania, 1787–1792, *Publius*, vol. 9, no. 2, Republicanism, Representation, and Consent: Views of the Founding Era (Spring, 1979) 123–37; Jackson Turner Main, The Antifederalists: Critics of the Constitution, 1781–1788, 2nd ed. (2004); Cecelia M. Kenyon, Men of Little Faith—The Antifederalists on the Nature of Representative Government, 12 *W.M. & MARY Q.* 3 (3d ser. 1955) 3–43, available https://faculty.uml.edu/sgallagher/Anti-Federalists.pdf; C. Wright Mills, The Power Elite (1959); Charles Beard, An Economic Interpretation of the Constitution of the United States (1913).

[58] As noted by Robert L. Clinton, "Elites have always concluded that ordinary people are incapable of governing themselves. Even so, however much a mess that ordinary people may make of the business of self-government, the fact remains that entitlement to rule cannot be taken from one on the basis of the intelligence quotient (IQ), experience,

role in the present political and legal process, in both rhetoric and application.[59] Elitism has and continues to play a substantive role in American politics, law, government, and governance. The Supreme Court, the most elite branch of the Federal Government, perhaps more so than the executive and the legislative branches, exercises profound power in articulating the fundamental law embodied in the Constitutional text through its assertion of judicial review and supremacy.[60] The Court, an unelected,

knowledge, or expertise of another. The threats to our constitutional democracy that we experience today are rooted in elitism, the belief that ordinary people are not really fit—and therefore are not entitled—to govern themselves, and that small groups of people 'in the know'—whether scientific, technological, economic, political, legal, or academic elites—can do a better job and are therefore entitled to do the governing for the rest of us." Robert L. Clinton, Democracy, the Supreme Court, and Our Two Constitutions, 8 *Faulkner L. Rev.* 1, 3 (2016).

[59] Cathleen Decker, "Trump's War Against Elites and Expertise," *LA Times*, July 27, 2017, available https://www.latimes.com/politics/la-na-pol-trump-elites-20170725-story.html. "Among his targets so far: the government's intelligence agencies, the media, foreign allies, the Department of Justice, establishment politicians, scientists and the Congressional Budget Office. The last has played a large role in raising questions about Republican proposals to repeal and replace Obamacare, leading to a furious White House assault on its competence. Trump has refused to accept the judgment of intelligence agencies that Russia interfered in the 2016 election. He has alleged, without proof and contrary to both Democratic and Republican officials in key states, that millions of illegal voters cast ballots last year. He has blamed vaccines for autism, despite the scientific debunking of that notion. Excoriating elites 'is classic populist language,' said Yale historian Beverly Gage. 'Trump has taken it to a whole new level by not only attacking clueless elites but the entire idea of expertise.' To voters listening for them, Trump's anti-elitism signals have blared. As telling as his political and policy postures is his language—who else but Trump would angrily call his predecessor's signature program 'a big fat ugly lie'—and a perpetual sense of victimization." Id.

[60] Judicial review is the "Authority [of the Court] to declare any act of Congress or of a state legislature void," because of its incompatibility (as defined by the Court) with the Constitution. Alpheus Thomas Mason, The Supreme Court: Palladium of Freedom (1962). Judicial supremacy signifies when judges exercise a monopoly on constitutional interpretation and meaning, in that judges "'hold the Constitution in one hand, and the law in the other, and say to the departments of Government, so far shall you go and no farther.'" Id. at 97. See *Marbury v. Madison*, 5 U.S. 137, 177–78 (1803) ("It is emphatically the province and duty of the judicial department to say what the law is. Those who apply the rule to particular cases, must of necessity expound and interpret that rule. If two laws conflict with each other, the courts must decide on the operation of each. So if a law be in opposition to the constitution; if both the law and the constitution apply to a particular case, so that the court must either decide that case conformably to the law, disregarding the constitution; or conformably to the constitution, disregarding the law; the court must determine which of these conflicting rules governs the case.

unaccountable, life-tenured institution whose members are all drawn from the upper echelon of elite academic institutions and elite professional work environments,[61] has given itself the formal power as final arbiter of constitutional meaning through review and supremacy. Irrespective of whether one believes the Supreme Court should exercise such power, it is the case that review and supremacy are based on an even more rudimentary political and legal ordering principle; i.e., elite control over government and governance.[62] MEF is thus useful for analyzing the Court's power because elitism is a consistent structural variable at work in constitutional order and interpretation. Elitism has and continues to figure prominently into the Supreme Court appointment process,[63] and it continues to find expression in the other two branches of government as well.[64]

This is of the very essence of judicial duty."); *Powell v. McCormack*, 395 U.S. 486, 549 (1969) ("[I]t is the responsibility of this Court to act as the ultimate interpreter of the Constitution."); *Baker v. Carr*, 369 U.S. 186, 211 (1962) ("[T]his Court [is the] ultimate interpreter of the Constitution."); *Cooper v. Aaron*, 358 U.S. 1, 18 (1958) ("[T]he federal judiciary is supreme in the exposition of the law of the Constitution ... It follows that the interpretation of the Fourteenth Amendment enunciated by this Court in the Brown case is the supreme law of the land, and Art. VI of the Constitution makes it of binding effect on the States.") See also Clinton, supra note 27; Michael Vitiello, How Imperial Is the Supreme Court—An Analysis of Supreme Court Abortion Doctrine and Popular Will, 34 *U.S.F. L. Rev.* 49 (1999); Joseph L. Call, Judicial Review vs. Judicial Supremacy, 62 *Dick. L. Rev.* 71 (1957); B. Jessie Hill, Resistance to Constitutional Theory: The Supreme Court, Constitutional Change, and the Pragmatic Moment, 91 *Tex. L. Rev.* 1815 (2013); *American Fed'n of Labor v. American Sash & Door Co.*, 335 U.S. 538, 556–57 (1949) (The Court's "right to pass on the validity of legislation is now too much part of our constitutional system to be brought into question").

[61] See Dave Sidhu, "Elitism and the Supreme Court," Jurist, May 20, 2010, available https://www.jurist.org/commentary/2010/05/elitism-and-the-supreme-court/#.

[62] See Mills, supra note 58. See also Dye, supra note 40.

[63] The "Roberts Court Justices have spent more pre-appointment time in legal academia, appellate judging, and living in Washington, DC, than any previous Supreme Court Justices. They also spent the most time in elite undergraduate and law school settings. Time spent in these pursuits has naturally meant less time spent elsewhere; the Roberts Court Justices have spent less time in the private practice of law, in trial judging, and as elected politicians than any previous Court." Benjamin H. Barton, An Empirical Study of Supreme Court Justice Pre-Appointment Experience, 64 *Fla. L. Rev.* 1137 (2012), available http://scholarship.law.ufl.edu/flr/vol64/iss5/1.

[64] See, e.g., James W. Riddlesperger and James D. King, Elitism and Presidential Appointments, *Social Science Quarterly*, vol. 70, no. 4 (December 1, 1989) 902; G. Lowell Field and John Higley, Elitism (1980).

Elitism, as MEF highlights, is an important factor to evaluate and elucidate because it has weighty consequences for representative democracy, viz., influencing the actual content and character of the people whom government ostensibly reflects and serves. In the case of judges and Justices, interpretation of the fundamental law and its application directly affect the people. Justice Marshall, dissenting in *U.S. v. Kras*,[65] and Chief Judge Kozinski, dissenting in *U.S. v. Pineda-Moreno*,[66] acknowledge a fundamental and crucial "difference between judges and most of their litigants: Judges overwhelmingly come from wealthy backgrounds, and many have never walked in the shoes of economically disadvantaged people."[67] MEF and LAPP thus help illuminate the consequences of a disconnected, nonrepresentational elite on law and society.

Structurally and systemically, the Court functions in a larger governmental schema underpinned by elitism in the realms of law, politics, economy, and society. Elitism in American politics and law, generally speaking, as articulated by its advocates and discontents, by those that hold themselves out as the paladins or antagonists of elitism and the elite in government, law, and the economy, explicitly informed the 2016 presidential election.[68] President Trump, ironically perhaps, in light of his socioeconomic class, campaigned and was elected president based, in part, on rhetoric and subsequent executive actions that have been premised on or appear to resonate with a mass as opposed to elite sentiment. The 2016 campaign emphasized a "populist" classification of the People rather than an elitist one. This "populist" posture has found rhetorical expression in the nomination of two Justices to the Court during Trump's tenure as

[65] 409 U.S. 460 (1973).

[66] 591 F.3d 1123 (9th Cir. 2010).

[67] Neitz, supra note 9 at 140.

[68] See Steven K. Bannon and David Frum, The Munk Debates: The Rise of Populism (2018). "When President Trump campaigned this spring at the Hermitage, the home of Andrew Jackson, one part of his predecessor's approach got a special endorsement. 'It was during the Revolution that Jackson first confronted and defied an arrogant elite. Does that sound familiar?' ... [F]or Trump and his allies, a war on elites has been central to the campaign which put him in the presidency and has maintained the loyalty of his core voters. Trump has taken particular aim at entities that could counter his power, which has helped stoke the ardor of his political backers." Decker, supra note 60.

president.[69] An in-depth analysis of populism is beyond the scope of this work. For the purpose of this analysis, it is sufficient to acknowledge that elitism has assumed a formative role in American law, society, and politics. Elites and an elitist perspective of government and governance have been operative since the founding of the American nation-state to safeguard the perpetuation and integrity of the American constitutional order—the basis for the American polity and the political and legal process that undergirds it, which also function as a repository for American identity.[70]

In the present, a crisis of American democracy, generally speaking, points to a profound existential challenge for the polity going forward. Elites and elite-management of public affairs and policy was explicitly put into play during the 2016 presidential election.[71] As mentioned previously, elitism in politics and law is certainly not a novel development.[72] Rather, what seems to be operative in the present American political and legal process is a politics of resentment, disconnectedness, polarization, fragmentation, and deep ideological fissures.[73] As Francis Fukuyama notes, some commentators contend that, in the twenty-first-

[69] See Joan Biskupic, Trump's 2020 Message Behind His Attacks on Liberal Supreme Court Justices, CNN, February 25, 2020, available https://www.cnn.com/2020/02/25/politics/trump-supreme-court-liberals/index.html.

[70] "Landholders ought to have a share in the government, to support these invaluable interests and to balance and check the other. They ought to be so constituted as to protect the minority of the opulent against the majority. The senate, therefore, ought to be this body; and to answer these purposes, they ought to have permanency and stability. Various have been the propositions; but my opinion is, the longer they continue in office, the better will these views be answered (Farrand, *Records*, I, 430–31)." "Term of the Senate, [26 June] 1787," Founders Online, National Archives, accessed September 29, 2019, available https://founders.archives.gov/documents/Madison/01-10-02-0044. [Original source: The Papers of James Madison, vol. 10, 27 May 1787–3 March 1788, ed. Robert A. Rutland, Charles F. Hobson, William M. E. Rachal, and Frederika J. Teute. Chicago: The University of Chicago Press, 1977, pp. 76–78.]

[71] Yasmeen Serhan, "Populism Is Morphing in Insidious Ways," *The Atlantic*, January 6, 2020, available https://www.theatlantic.com/international/archive/2020/01/future-populism-2020s/604393/.

[72] "Whatever the type of political organization, pressures arising from the discontent of the masses who are governed, from the passions by which they are swayed, exert a certain amount of influence on the policies of the ruling, the political, class." Mosca, supra note 51 at 51.

[73] See William Davies, "Why We Stopped Trusting Elites," *The Guardian*, November 29, 2018, available https://www.theguardian.com/news/2018/nov/29/why-we-stopped-trusting-elites-the-new-populism.

century public policy "crafted by elites [seems to have] produced huge recessions, high unemployment, and falling incomes for millions of ordinary workers."[74] Whether or not this specific contention is true is a separate issue from highlighting the role elitism assumes in the legal and political process and in the manufacture of public policy. Elites, in the present, or so it seems, are doing an ineffective job in quelling, managing, and resolving the multifarious crises that the American polity is experiencing. Presently, it seems that the American people are ensnared in "the violent paroxysms of a collective identity in crisis ... People kill for culture ... Language, race, religion, blood, myth, history, national codes, and manners have all been used ... in the US ... to enforce terror, to 'otherize ...' questions such as who is an American and what is American culture are being posed with belligerence and being answered with violence."[75]

In light of the role MEF and LAPP have and continue to assume in broadly framing American politics and law, is the Court, perhaps the most elitist branch of government, directly or indirectly affecting the volatility that seems to permeate American government and identity? As elite managers of constitutional discourse, how does the Court contribute to the present state of politics? The Court's jurisprudence can be viewed within MEF and LAPP as far as the sociocultural, political, and economic character of the Court, and its place and function in the constitutional structure/order.[76] In the case of immigration law and policy, for instance,

[74] Francis Fukuyama, Against Identity Politics: The New Tribalism and the Crisis of Democracy, *Foreign Affairs*, September/October (2018), available https://www.foreignaffairs.com/articles/americas/2018-08-14/against-identity-politics-tribalism-francis-fukuyama. See also Michael J. Sandel, Public Philosophy: Essays on Morality in Politics (2005) 12–16.

[75] Bharati Mukherjee, "Beyond Multiculturalism," in Multi-America: Essays on Cultural Wars & Cultural Peace 455–57 (ed. Ishmael Reed, 1998). There appears to be a "growing fear, that, individually and collectively, we are less and less in control of the forces that govern our lives. Despite the extension of rights and entitlements in recent decades, and despite the expansion of the franchise, Americans increasingly [seem] to find themselves in the grip of impersonal structures of power that defy their understanding and control." See also Sandel, supra note 75 at 37.

[76] See William Wan, "Every Current Supreme Court Justice Attended Harvard or Yale. That's a Problem, Say Decision-Making Experts," *Washington Post*, July 11, 2018, available https://www.washingtonpost.com/news/speaking-of-science/wp/2018/07/11/every-supreme-court-justice-attended-harvard-or-yale-thats-a-problem-say-decision-making-experts/. "[W]e find many activities carried through the governing body without

the Court has been called to rule upon the constitutionality of public policy put forth by the executive that has had the effect of pitting the executive against the lower federal courts in defining who is or can be an American, and having the courts and the Court make determinations that some have contended are purely ideological in nature.[77] Recent Court rulings have, apparently, had the effect of bolstering while concomitantly undermining the Trump Administration's exclusionary immigration policy.[78]

MEF, in conjunction with LAPP as discussed in the following chapters, provides insight into the Court's role, its affect and effect, on the overarching political and legal process. More specifically, each provides insight as to how the Court's elitist nature has and continues to impact the larger political and legal process via the legal construct of the People.

the direct appearance on the scene of the underlying groups through representation by differentiated activities of a political character. And yet those underlying activities are actually supporting and indirectly 'making' the law that results. And what is more, however indirect the process of making may seem to be, through whatever complicated technical elements of representation or control it works, the law once made is just as much as in the former case supported by the group activity and group interest. It has no meaning without reference to that activity, and it is fundamentally that activity's creation and that activity's legal functioning, whatever its technical mediation." Arthur F. Bentley, The Process of Government 290-291 (1908).

[77] See Clark, supra note 51; *Hawaii v. Trump*, 859 F.3d 741, 768–69 (9th Cir. 2017); *Sarsour v. Trump*, 245 F. Supp. 3d 719 (E.D. Va. 2017); Int'l Refugee Assistance Project v. Trump, 857 F.3d 554 (4th Cir. 2017) (citations omitted), vacated, 153 S. Ct. 353; Aziz v. Trump, 234 F. Supp. 3d 724 (E.D. Va. 2017); Kevin Liptak, Daniella Diaz and Sophie Tatum, Trump Pardons Former Sheriff Joe Arpaio, CNN (August 27, 2017), available http://www.cnn.com/2017/08/25/politics/sheriff-joe-arpaio-donald-trump-pardon/index.html; Justice Thomas, writing separately in *Trump v. International Refugee Assistance Project*, 582 U. S. _ (2017), noted that, the "[g]overnment has also established that failure to stay the injunctions will cause irreparable harm by interfering with its 'compelling need to provide for the Nation's security.' Finally, weighing the Government's interest in preserving national security against the hardships caused to respondents by temporary denials of entry into the country, the balance of the equities favors the Government. I would thus grant the Government's applications for a stay in their entirety."

[78] See, e.g., *Dept. of Homeland Sec. v. Thuraissigiam*, 591 U. S. __ (2020) (19-161, 2020 WL 3454809 [U.S. June 25, 2020]) (holding that the federal statute limiting habeas review in expedited-removal proceedings does not violate the Suspension Clause, and that an alien lacked constitutional procedural due process right to judicial review of negative credible-fear determination) *Dept. of Homeland Sec. v. Regents of the U. of California*, 591 U.S. ___ (2020) (18-587, 2020 WL 3271746 [U.S. June 18, 2020]) (finding that the executive's rescission of DACA program was arbitrary and capricious).

The People, this work contends, when filtered through the prism of Court power, is a legal-political construct with ideological underpinnings that directly effects representative democratic politics. The construct of the People in the Court's jurisprudence is one of the Court's making, which enables Court power to manifest in government and governance.

Since the inception of the Constitution, the Court has undergone a process of interjecting itself into the realm of policymaking through the interpretive enterprise. In the twentieth and twenty-first centuries, the Court has profoundly impacted the character and content of Constitutional order.[79] Since 1938, the Court, after disengaging from economic policy oversight,[80] explicitly interjected itself into the sociopolitical and sociocultural realms of public policy via interpretation of the fundamental law.[81] MEF and LAPP thus have explanatory power when attempting to identify and assess the socioeconomic and political dynamics and consequentialness of Court power within the overarching context of American government and governance.[82] This is especially the case when

[79] See *United States v. Carolene Products*, 304 U.S. 144, 155 n.4 (1938) (positing that "discrete and insular minorities" may require heightened judicial attention and protection).

[80] See, e.g., *Lochner v. New York*, 198 U.S. 45 (1905) (finding that statutory limits to the amount of an individual's working time violated the Fourteenth Amendment).

[81] *United States v. Carolene Products*, 304 U.S. 144, 155 n.4 (1938)

[82] The Justices have been referred to "Politicians in Robes ... researchers found that, when casting a pivotal vote, liberal justices are more likely to vote liberally while conservatives are more likely to vote conservatively, compared to when those same judges cast a non-pivotal vote. In short, justices vote differently when they realize that their vote really matters. And the pattern becomes more pronounced for justices who are more ideologically extreme. The researchers found that the more liberal or conservative a justice is, the more frequently he or she votes in that direction when casting the deciding vote." Tom Clark, B. Pablo Montagnes, and Jörg L. Spenkuch, "Supreme Court Justices Become Less Impartial and More Ideological When Casting the Swing Vote," Northwestern University, Kellogg School of Management, September 13, 2018, available https://insight.kellogg.northwestern.edu/article/supreme-court-justices-become-less-impartial-and-more-ideological-when-casting-the-swing-vote. See also Eden E. Torres, Power, Politics, and Pleasure: Class Differences and the Law, 54 *Rutgers L. Rev.* 853, 863 (2002); Neitz, supra note 9 at 142: "Judicial salaries are much higher than those earned by average Americans. Nearly all state and federal judges in the United States earn a six figure salary. For example, in 2010, district court judges earned a set salary of $174,000, and circuit court judges made $184,000. Supreme Court justices make over $200,000. Depending on the jurisdiction, state court judges may make more or less than federal judges. For example, state appellate judges earn salaries ranging from $105,050 in Mississippi (the state with the lowest paid state appellate judges) to $204,599 in California (the state boasting the highest salaries for its appellate judges). In 2010, the median

considering how the Court has imagined the People in articulating and declaring the fundamental law for all that reside under the Constitution's jurisdiction. According to the Court, "The Constitution … creates a uniform national body representing the interests of a single people."[83] Yet, through judicial review and supremacy, premised, in part, on the People, the Court has granted itself the ultimate and singular power to determine the contours and parameters of what exactly constitutes constitutional thought, and the potential limits and possibilities of subjects under the fundamental law.

household income was $49,445.29 Thus, judges earn more than double the income of the average American. Like all people, judges are influenced by their economic backgrounds." Id.

[83] *U.S. Term Limits, Inc. v. Thornton*, 514 U.S. 779, 822 (1995).

CHAPTER 2

Step 2: Illuminating Court Power Through Disaggregation—Elitism, Power, Process, Discourse and Representation

Abstract The elitist nature of the Court has profound implications for representative democracy. It is a nondemocratic, life-tenured, unaccountable institution composed of nine people that constitute a highly discrete and insular institution, and who occupy positions at the highest echelons of the sociocultural and economic sectors of society. Nine judges determine constitutional reality for 330 million people. The Court's identity and interests play a key role in the overarching constitutional order and interpretation of the fundamental law through judicial review and supremacy. The Court has exercised profound power through its singular interpretation of the fundamental law, creating a corpus of law which functions as a lodestar and ballast for maintaining the integrity, stability, authority, and legitimacy of the constitutional order that underpins the polity. The sociopolitical and economic consequences of the Court's notion of the People, as a medium by which the Court legitimates its position, role, and authority, are examined.

Keywords Judicial review · Judicial supremacy · Mass/elite · Law-as-process · Rule of law

M. L. Astrada, *Law, Society & Politics*,
https://doi.org/10.1007/978-3-030-66714-6_2

Since the tenure of Chief Justice Marshall (1801–1835) through the present, the Supreme Court has explicitly tasked itself with substantially augmenting the power of the Court and the federal government over the States and the peoples, and maintaining the integrity of its power and constitutional order through the exercise of judicial review and supremacy. This is noteworthy because the Court's characterization of the power of "Congress, which came into existence, and exists, only by virtue of the Constitution, [and] can withhold fundamental guarantees of life and liberty from peoples," applies to Court power as well.[1] The Court has over time refined the process whereby the concept of the People serves as an instrumentation to convert the peoples into the People. In *McCulloch v. Maryland*,[2] for instance, the Court declared that "government proceeds directly from the people; is 'ordained and established,' in the name of the people; and is declared to be ordained, 'in order to form a more perfect union, establish justice, insure domestic tranquility, and secure the blessings of liberty to themselves and to their posterity.'" In *McCulloch*, the Court privileges and reifies the Peoples as the basis of the American polity and not the States, which were the original repositories of the variegated peoples that constituted the fledging republic. "The assent of the states, in their sovereign capacity, is implied, in calling a convention, and thus submitting that instrument to the people. But the people were at perfect liberty to accept or reject it; and their act was final. It required not the affirmance, and could not be negatived, by the state governments. The constitution, when thus adopted, was of complete obligation, and bound the state sovereignties"[3] In positing the preeminence of the People of the American nation over that of the constituent local State-based peoples, the Court in *McCulloch* embedded its political, normative, ideological, sociocultural and socioeconomic worldview into the Constitution—one based, in part, on a politicized identity-based interpretation of the American People, viewing federal power as emanating from "We the People" and not "We the States."[4] The Court privileges Union over

[1] *Territory of Hawaii v. Mankichi*, 190 U.S. 197, 236 (1903).

[2] 17 U.S. 316, 403–404 (1819).

[3] *McCulloch v. Maryland*, 17 U.S. 316, 403–404 (1819).

[4] Louise Weinberg, Of Sovereignty and the Union: The Legends of Alden, 76 *NOTRE DAME L. REV*. 1113, 1150 (2001). See also Christopher L. Eisgruber, The Fourteenth Amendment's Constitution, 69 *S. CAL. L. REV*. 47, 66 (1995) ("Marshall treated the American people as a single entity incapable of making a binding agreement with itself.").

diversity as far as how the peoples are to be construed in the fundamental law, even though the Court admits that, "No political dreamer was ever wild enough to think of breaking down the lines which separate the States, *and of compounding the American people into one common mass*."[5] Yet, the People, as interpreted by the Court is antipodal to the foregoing in thought and practice.

Over time, the Court has exercised its power of review and supremacy, in part, in the form of checks and balances and separation of powers over both the federal and state governments—each being a key facet of Court power and identity.[6] The elite Justices that populate the Court, as well as the groups that come before the Court seeking its judgment, can be classified as embodying group-based interests possessing a degree of identarian underpinnings.[7] The elitist nature of the Court is explicitly reflected in its place in the constitutional order and its character. It is a nondemocratic, life-tenured, unaccountable institution composed of nine people that constitute a highly discrete and insular institution, and who occupy positions at the highest echelons of the sociocultural and

"But the constitution acts directly on the people, by means of powers communicated directly from the people. No state, in its corporate capacity, ratified it; but it was proposed for adoption to popular conventions. It springs from the people, precisely as the state constitution springs from the people, and acts on them in a similar manner. It was adopted by them in the geographical sections into which the country is divided. The federal powers are just as sovereign as those of the states. The state sovereignties are not the authors of the constitution of the United States. They are preceding in point of time, to the national sovereignty, but they are postponed to it, in point of supremacy, by the will of the people." McCulloch v. Maryland, 17 U.S. 316, 377–78 (1819).

[5] McCulloch v. Maryland, 17 U.S. 316, 403 (1819).

[6] See Otis H. Jr. Stephens, John Marshall and the Confluence of Law and Politics, 71 *Tenn. L. Rev.* 241 (2004); Martin Shapiro, The Impact of Supreme Court Decisions: The Supreme Court Speaks & What Happens? 23 *J. Legal Educ.* 77 (1970–1971), available https://scholarship.law.berkeley.edu/cgi/viewcontent.cgi?article=1518&context=facpubs.

[7] See William J. Daniels, The Supreme Court and Its Publics, 37 *Alb. L. Rev.* 632 (1973); P. M. Williams, The Supreme Court and Politics, 5 *Oxford J. Legal Stud.* 91 (1985).

economic sectors of society.[8] The nine "brethren"[9] of the Court determine constitutional reality for 330 million people. The Court's identity[10] and interests[11] thus play a key role in the overarching constitutional order

[8] See Arthur F. Bentley, The Process of Government 288-289 (1908). "[A]ll law strikes at something. That something will inevitably be human activity. This is only to put in other language the principle of the group interpretation itself. Any classification of laws into those which hit at evils and those which work constructively for public welfare is fundamentally wrong, or, rather, it pretends to be fundamental, when actually it is superficial ... I do not want to be understood, however, as saying that this is the only point of view, or for all purposes the best point of view, to take of the phenomena. Activity is very positive from the point of view of the actors. The striking done by the law is not anything negative which exists merely for striking's sake. But it is never, on the other hand, a pure matter of everybody's welfare. However much any of it may be ennobled and glorified in the speech that accompanies and represents it, the conflict phase can be found when the whole range of the society in which it exists is taken into account. For its interpretation the discovery of this phase is essential." Id.

[9] Bob Woodward and Scott Armstrong, The Brethren: Inside the Supreme Court Paperback (1979).

[10] See Rogers M. Smith, "Identities, Interests, and the Future of Political Science, *Perspectives on Politics*, vol. 2, no. 2 (June, 2004) 301–12, 302. Identity "is the 'collective aspect of the set of characteristics by which a thing is definitively recognizable or known . . . The set of behavioral or personal characteristics by which a person is recognizable as a member of a group.' By extension, a political identity can be conceived as the collective label for a set of characteristics by which persons are recognized by political actors as members of a political group ...We can define 'political actors' and 'political groups,' in turn, as those people who determine how governing power will be created, distributed, exercised, and ended, in ways that partly decide, among other things, who gets what, when, and how. A person's political identities—since individuals have many characteristics and group memberships, they usually possess more than one identity—indicate the populations with which political actors expect that person to be affiliated in contests over governing power and its use ... political identities are important realities in human experience." Id.

[11] Gaetano Mosca, The Ruling Class, Hannah D. Kahn ed. & trans. (1939). 114 "The fact is that the human being has sentiments which, taken individually, may be imponderable, hard to analyze and harder still to define, but which in sum are very powerful and may contribute to bringing on the most important social phenomena. The person who wrote that the human being lets himself be guided by self-interest alone stated a general maxim that is almost entirely devoid of practical value, since it can tell us nothing save at the cost of exceedingly minute analyses and distinctions. Anyone who thinks that interest has to be something that can be expressed materially in terms of money and measured in pounds and pence is a person of too little heart and too little head to understand the people about him. Interest is suited in each individual to the individual's own tastes, and each individual interprets his interest in his own individual way. For many people, to satisfy their pride, their sense of personal dignity, their vanities great and small, to humor their personal caprices and rancors [sic], is worth far more than pleasures that are

and interpretation of the fundamental law. The Court has claimed, explicitly and implicitly, the power of judicial review and judicial supremacy.[12] These powers, in part, have enabled the Court, in its words, to "discover" and "obtain keys with which to open the mind of the people, and discover the thought intended to be expressed" in the fundamental law.[13] The Court has exercised profound power through its singular interpretation of the fundamental law, creating a corpus of law which functions as a lodestar and ballast for maintaining the integrity, stability, authority, and legitimacy of the constitutional order that underpins the polity.[14]

In light of MEF, which highlights the binary that generally structures the distribution of power to substantially affect and effect the legal and political process, how does LAPP enhance the capacity to obtain insight and gauge the Court's power and its effects on the character and content of law, politics, and society? What exactly constitutes LAPP, and how does it complement MEF? The Court's relationship with the fundamental law and ROL is one that helps sustain the United States as a sociocultural, economic, and political unit. LAPP thus perceives law *in* and *as* government; this has significant implications for the interpretation of law by a supreme judicial Authority that is nondemocratic, life-tenured, and nonrepresentational, and its relationship to the people via the People.[15]

purely material. We must not forget such things, especially when we set out to analyze the relations between rich and poor, between superiors and inferiors, or, in short, between different social classes." Id. Note that, while Mosca may be mistaken or rather exaggerating the power of the individual to set his own interests, it is nonetheless the case that that interests(s) must be viewed much more expansively than mere materially-based phenomenon. Interests(s) is what political identity helps produce and is a product of, furthering the ideological, political, economic, and sociocultural agendas that underpin it via elite representatives.

[12] See Barry Friedman, The History of the Counter-majoritarian Difficulty, Part One: The Road to Judicial Supremacy, 73 *N.Y.U. L. REV*. 333 (1998); Edward A. Hartnett, A Matter of Judgment, Not a Matter of Opinion, 74 *N.Y.U. L. REV*. 123 (1999); Larry D. Kramer, Foreword: We the Court, 115 *HARV. L. REV*. 4, 6–16 (2001).

[13] *Civil Rights Cases*, 109 U.S. 3, 28 (1883).

[14] See William W. Van Alstyne, Idea of the Constitution as Hard Law, 37 *J. Legal Educ.* 174 (1987); Larry Alexander, The Constitution as Law, 6 *Const. Comment*. 103 (1989); Raoul Berger, Constitutional Law and the Constitution, 19 *Suffolk U. L. Rev*. 1 (1985).

[15] Law-as-process, Bentley observes, includes:

A. The written rule printed in statute book or volume of precedents, accompanied most often by written interpretations handed down by the courts.
B. The plaintiff and the defendant.

LAPP views the Court as an extension of overall government, not a mythic institution ensconced in a Greek temple divorced from the political process. It considers the sociocultural dimension of law, broadly defined, to include material and intangible states of affairs, such as politics, ideology, philosophy, and economic thought, that play a profound role in the interpretation of the fundamental law, and consequently the ordering of society and the identity of the peoples and the People in a representative democracy. "Law matches government every inch of its course. The two are not different things but the same thing. We cannot call law a resultant of government. Rather we must say it is government that same phenomenon only, stated from a different angle ... Law is activity, just as government is. It is a group process, just as government is. It is a forming, a systematization, a struggle, an adaptation, of group interests, just as government is."[16] Law thus constitutes an expansive and processual state of affairs. It is far more than the mere technical exercise of formulating and applying rules governing conduct. The "'law of a society is something beyond the sum of its laws.' What that common manner of statement means is merely that the process of summation is not the

C. The activity of one portion of the population, probably very large, along the lines prescribed, or, better said, described, in the written text.
D. The activity of another portion of the population, probably very small, along lines conflicting with those described by the written law.
E. In the background, the activity of some law-registering body, legislature, or court, our authority for the text.
F. The activity of a set of officials, including public prosecutors, who seek with greater or less energy the persons whose activity deviates from the line set forth in certain parts of this law and who bring them before courts.
G. The activity of certain persons, the lawyers in private practice, who represent persons who do conform to the habit in the effort to penalize others who do not conform; also, the activity of those same lawyers in representing those who do not conform.
H. The activity of a set of persons, the judges, who measure conformity or nonconformity, declare it in formal terms, and impose penalties.
I. The activities of a set of persons who execute penalties or enforce decrees.
J. The activities of a set of persons who, placing themselves at various points in the process, and allying themselves with various groupings, reflect or represent the tendencies of the groups in various degrees of completeness through spoken or written language. Bentley, supra note 8 at 275.

[16] Id. at 272. See also Mario L. Barnes and Erwin Chemerinsky, The Disparate Treatment of Race and Class in Constitutional Jurisprudence, 72 *LAW & CONTEMP. PROBS.* 109, 111 (2009).

process which will give us an adequate picture of the whole body of the law. And the reason summation is inadequate lies in the abstract, and hence artificial, nature of the components which it is attempted to add together. It is not merely laws but rather systems of law with which we actually have to deal."[17]

Law as process can be restated as law as activity. Because law is activity, it is empirical—it constitutes and is constitutive of physical behavior. Law is also ideational—comprised of abstractions that animate behavior, such as norms, values, and ideology. Both are amenable to critical analysis at a systemic level. Although Bentley articulated his conceptual process-based framework over a century ago, nonetheless it retains its validity, application, because of the fundamental premise that undergirds it, viz., the notion that law is activity-based. All human enterprises are rooted in activity. The nouns that provide guideposts (signifieds) for defining a society, such as Justice, Equality, and Rule of Law, are also verbs, actions, in that each guidepost is a signifier constituted via activity. The activity-based character of LAPP thus renders it relevant as a working lens by which to acquire insight and ascertain the consequentialness of Court power in the Constitutional order and on democratic politics and society. "[I]f we hold to the view that all law is itself activity, we have no reason for wandering off into the mysteries, or preferring the least stable to the most stable elements in our explanation. It is of the very definition of activity that it is systematized ... [Law] is a representative activity, reflecting certain group interests along certain lines."[18] Activity and groups, viz., elites and the mass, are therefore key to explaining and understanding the role of law and its impact on democratic representative politics. LAPP complements MEF in explicating the relationship between activity, groups, identity, and representative government. Each helps to reveal the nuances, complexity, and consequentialness betwixt law as activity, groups, and representative government and politics. Justices of the Court constitute a group-based interest in promulgating law, and the Court also deals with and accommodates competing elite interests that are brought before it. The law thus reflects the complex interaction between group interests, activity, and politics.

[17] Bentley, supra note 8 at 284.

[18] Bentley, supra note 8 at 285.

LAPP not only sheds light on the ideological, sociocultural, and political nature of the Court, but also provides insight into the structural ordering mechanisms—both ideational and empirical—that directly impact the representativeness of government.[19] Although ROL is the basis upon which Court power is legitimated and made authoritative,[20] rules, regulations, and law are products and producers of activity, which are permeated by interests that find expression in groups. Law encompasses so much more than "reasoned elaboration,"[21] the

> passive discovery of a repository of principles and rights that are representative of and rooted in impersonal principles … positioning the study of law

[19] "[I]n any human aggregate which has attained a certain level of civilization a ruling minority exists, and that this minority is recruited in ways that may vary but that are always based upon the possession of multiple and variable social forces in other words, of those qualities or resources which give moral prestige and intellectual and economic preeminence to the individuals who possess them … every society is founded upon a complex of religious and philosophical beliefs and principles which are peculiar to it and by which it explains and justifies the type of organization that it happens to have." Mosca, supra note 11 at 244.

[20] See *Boddie v. Connecticut*, 401 U.S. 371, 374–75 (1971). "Perhaps no characteristic of an organized and cohesive society is more fundamental than its erection and enforcement of a system of rules defining the various rights and duties of its members, enabling them to govern their affairs and definitively settle their differences in an orderly, predictable manner. Without such a 'legal system,' social organization and cohesion are virtually impossible; with the ability to seek regularized resolution of conflicts individuals are capable of interdependent action that enables them to strive for achievements without the anxieties that would beset them in a disorganized society. Put more succinctly, it is this injection of the rule of law that allows society to reap the benefits of rejecting what political theorists call the 'state of nature.' American society, of course, bottoms its systematic definition of individual rights and duties, as well as its machinery for dispute settlement, not on custom or the will of strategically placed individuals, but on the common-law model. It is to courts, or other quasi-judicial official bodies, that we ultimately look for the implementation of a regularized, orderly process of dispute settlement. Within this framework, those who wrote our original Constitution, in the Fifth Amendment, and later those who drafted the Fourteenth Amendment recognized the centrality of the concept of due process in the operation of this system. Without this guarantee that one may not be deprived of his rights, neither liberty nor property, without due process of law, the State's monopoly over techniques for binding conflict resolution could hardly be said to be acceptable under our scheme of things. Only by providing that the social enforcement mechanism must function strictly within these bounds can we hope to maintain an ordered society that is also just. It is upon this premise that this Court has through years of adjudication put flesh upon the due process principle." Id.

[21] See, e.g., Roberto Mangabeira Unger, The Critical Legal Studies Movement: Another Time, A Greater Task (1983) 5.

> as an 'uncovering' of social purpose for various legal concepts, correlated with an idealized 'purity' of the law outside of the politics of legislation and historical context ... Law is far from being divorced from the politics that permeate the constructs and principles of social organization; rather, law is fraught with politics, and reflects a fluid and evolving ulterior state of affairs ... The same tension between objectivity and subjectivity exists between the ostensible clarity of the interpretation and end result of law.[22]

When the Court renders judgment, when it "finds," reconfigures, or ablates the fundamental law, it is engaged in a process whereby judgment, to some degree, modifies the "facts" on which it is passed, revisited, reconfigured, or dispensed with.[23] Judgment is activity, process, underpinned by assorted, competing interests.[24] Judgment, while devoid of objective criteria per se, is a form of (political) thought that is itself a form of (political) action.[25]

The political dimension of judgment is less about particular categorizations, such as "left" and "right,"[26] than about the shifting, layered,

[22] Marvin L. Astrada and Scott B. Astrada, Law, Continuity & Change: Revisiting the Reasonable Person Within the Demographic, Sociocultural & Political Realities of the 21st Century, 14 *Rutgers J. L. & Pub. Pol'y* 201 (2017), available http://www.rutgerspolicyjournal.org/sites/jlpp/files/Astrada.pdf.

[23] See E.H. Carr, The Twenty Years Crisis (1976) 1–10.

[24] See, e.g., *Citizens United v. Federal Election Commission*, 558 U.S. 310 (2010) (wherein the Court found that the free speech under the First Amendment prohibits government from restricting independent expenditures for political communications by corporations, including nonprofit corporations, labor unions, and other associations); *Obergefell v. Hodges*, 576 U.S. ___ (2015) (wherein the Court found that a fundamental right to marry is guaranteed to same-sex couples by both the Due Process Clause and the Equal Protection Clause of the Fourteenth Amendment). Both cases are exemplars of elite group activity and interests finding constitutional expression via 5–4 decisions, which, in turn, reflects the internal group interests, dynamics, and ideological and political predispositions of the Court's personnel. Each of the cases came about because elite group-based interests on the "right" and the "left" sought the Court's imprimatur of constitutionality on their respective policy positions.

[25] Carr, supra note 23 at 8.

[26] See, e.g., Kevin T. McGuire, et al., Measuring Policy Content on the U.S. Supreme Court, *The Journal of Politics*, vol. 71, no. 4 (October 2009) 1305–21; Michael A. Bailey, "Measuring Ideology on the Courts" in The Routledge Handbook of Judicial Behavior, eds. Robert M. Howard and Kirk A. Randazzo (2017).

and relative bases upon which the true and the real are premised.[27] The lexis of Court power, i.e., mode of representation,[28] because it is activity-based and informed by group interests, is infused with sociality and thus operates on a relative as opposed to objective plane.[29] Judgment can, therefore, be viewed as an act of imagination; imagination enables the power to invent criteria for "objective" judgment.[30] Alexander Hamilton may indeed have severely underestimated the power of judgment rooted in imagination.[31] The purlieus of judgment are left to the discretion of the authority that adjudges, and its estimation as far as the political and social capital it has when rendering verdicts that interpret the character and content of the People. For instance, the "freedom secured by the Constitution is inherently unstable because there is no fixed stopping point to the [restriction of or] demand for it: Progress in enlarging freedom's realm provides new desires and reasons for further enlargement ... progress in enlarging freedom's realm creates new threats—including the temptation to adopt illiberal and antidemocratic measures—to the preservation of the order that the peaceful enjoyment and wise exercise of freedom requires."[32] Thus, the Court can state that, "No political

[27] "A doctrine is a thread by which those who are examining a given body of facts try to guide themselves in the maze which the facts seem to present at first glance; and a doctrine becomes the more useful in practice the more it facilitates and simplifies the understanding and analysis of facts. In this matter of political theory, as in so many other matters, appearances are often as satisfactory to people as the substance would be." Mosca, supra note 11 at 336.

[28] Jean Francois Lyotard and Jean-Loup Thebaud, Just Gaming, trans. Wlad Godzich (1999) 5.

[29] See, e.g., the Court's analysis of the People vis-à-vis due process of law in *Davidson v. City of New Orleans*, 96 U.S. 97, 107–8 (1877). ("Such an examination may be made without interfering with that large discretion which every legislative power has of making wide modifications in the forms of procedure in each case, according as the laws, habits, customs, and preferences of the people of the particular State may require.").

[30] Lyotard, "Gaming," supra 26 at 17–18.

[31] See Hamilton, infra note 57.

[32] Peter Berkowitz, "The Court, the Constitution, and the Culture of Freedom," Policy Review, Hoover Institute, Stanford University (August and September 2005), available https://www.hoover.org/research/court-constitution-and-culture-freedom. See, e.g., *Loving v. Virginia*, 388 U.S. 1, 12 (1967) (marriage based on personal freedom); *Skinner v. Oklahoma*, 316 U.S. 535, 541–42 (1942) (procreation based on personal freedom); *Eisenstadt v. Baird*, 405 U.S. 438, 453–54, 460, 463–65 (1972) (White, J., concurring in result) (contraception based on personal freedom); *Prince v. Massachusetts*, 321 U.S.

dreamer was ever wild enough to think of breaking down the lines which separate the states, and of compounding the American people into one common mass,"[33] even though this is exactly what the Court does when it posits the People in its constitutional discourse.

Although law characterizes government, and government is political and ideological in nature, the Court continues to espouse the myth of judicial independence and being apolitical. "There is[, however,] nothing mysterious about law; but the task of unraveling its group intricacies without indulging in an appeal to mysteries is as difficult as any task we have to face. One trouble with the analysis lies in the many kinds of facts the word law indicates, in the many meanings it has, even when no attention is paid to any meanings other than those found in connection with the phenomena of government."[34] Chief Justice Roberts' rebuke of President Trump's comments about his displeasure with an "Obama judge" highlights the enduring myth of judicial independence, its apolitical stature in American law, society, and politics. The Chief Justice stated that, "We do not have Obama judges or Trump judges, Bush judges or Clinton judges ... What we have is an extraordinary group of dedicated judges doing their level best to do equal right to those appearing before

158, 166 (1944) (family relationships based on personal freedom); (child rearing and education based on personal freedom) *Pierce v. Society of Sisters*, 268 U.S. 510, 535 (1925) (family relationships based on personal freedom). In the case of due process, a fundamental concept that the Court has utilized to expand its reach into the lives of its subjects, the Court has declared that, "'Due process has not been reduced to any formula; its content cannot be determined by reference to any code. The best that can be said is that through the course of this Court's decisions it has represented the balance which our Nation, built upon postulates of respect for the liberty of the individual, has struck between that liberty and the demands of organized society. If the supplying of content to this Constitutional concept has of necessity been a rational process, it certainly has not been one where judges have felt free to roam where unguided speculation might take them. The balance of which I speak is the balance struck by this country, having regard to what history teaches are the traditions from which it developed as well as the traditions from which it broke. That tradition is a living thing. A decision of this Court which radically departs from it could not long survive, while a decision which builds on what has survived is likely to be sound. No formula could serve as a substitute, in this area, for judgment and restraint.'" *Poe v. Ullman*, 367 U.S., at 542, 81 S.Ct., at 1776 (opinion dissenting from dismissal on jurisdictional grounds). See also *Planned Parenthood of Se. Pennsylvania v. Casey*, 505 U.S. 833, 849–50 (1992).

[33] *McCulloch v. Maryland*, 17 U.S. 316, 403 (1819).

[34] Bentley, supra note 8 at 272.

them. That independent judiciary is something we should all be thankful for."[35] Despite this assertion, Thomas Jefferson notes that,

> To consider the judges as the ultimate arbiters of all constitutional questions [is] a very dangerous doctrine indeed, and one which would place us under the despotism of an oligarchy. Our judges are as honest as other men and not more so. They have with others the same passions for party, for power, and the privilege of their corps. Their maxim is boni judicis est ampliare jurisdictionem [good justice is broad jurisdiction], and their power the more dangerous as they are in office for life and not responsible, as the other functionaries are, to the elective control. The Constitution has erected no such single tribunal, knowing that to whatever hands confided, with the corruptions of time and party, its members would become despots. It has more wisely made all the departments co-equal and co-sovereign within themselves.[36]

Jefferson's sentiment reflects a concern for the potential usurpation of power inherent in a branch of the national government independent of democratically established executive and legislative power and hegemony.[37] The judiciary, some commentators claim, cannot become or be too independent in that it becomes a "despotic oligarchy," but it must be sufficiently independent that it remains, in James Madison's words, an "impenetrable bulwark" against the exercise of authority not delegated to the other branches or reserved to the states, as well as against unjustified infringements on civil liberties and rights.[38] Therefore, an inherent

[35] Editorial Board, "John Roberts Said There Are No Trump Judges or Obama Judges," *Washington Post*, June 28, 2019, available https://www.washingtonpost.com/opinions/john-roberts-said-there-are-no-trump-judges-or-obama-judges-clarence-thomas-didnt-get-the-memo/2019/06/28/00ec5db0-99c6-11e9-8d0a-5edd7e2025b1_story.html.

[36] Thomas Jefferson to William C. Jarvis, 1820. ME 15:277, Landmark Cases of the Supreme Court, available https://www.landmarkcases.org/marbury-v-madison/thomas-jeffersons-reaction.

[37] For an opposing view, see Thomas I. Vanaskie, The Independence and Responsibility of the Federal Judiciary, 46 *Vill. L. Rev.* 745, 746 (2001).

[38] Id. at 745–46. Note Jefferson's view that, "The Constitution . . . meant that its coordinate branches should be checks on each other. But the opinion which gives to the judges the right to decide what laws are constitutional and what not, not only for themselves in their own sphere of action but for the Legislature and Executive also in their spheres, would make the Judiciary a despotic branch." Thomas Jefferson to Abigail Adams, 1804. ME 11:51. Jefferson, supra note 34. See Larry Alexander and Frederick

tension arises in a democratic context from having the Court assign itself the power of review and supremacy as to what the fundamental law ultimately means. The process that underpins Court power is different from the other branches because, while it functions in a larger MEF context like the others, it functions differently in its specific exercise of power as ultimate and singular interpreter of the fundamental law. This is the case, in part, because review and supremacy, ideological predispositions aside, attenuate the "products of direct democracy," such as State ballot initiatives being more reflective of representative democracy than the Court's pronouncements.[39]

While voluminous arguments have been made extolling the virtues of an elitist Court or pointing out its deficiencies,[40] it is the case that,

Schauer, Defending Judicial Supremacy: A Reply, 17 *CONST. COMMENT*. 455 (2000); Rachel E. Barkow, More Supreme Than Court? The Fall of the Political Question Doctrine and the Rise of Judicial Supremacy, 102 *COLUM. L. REV*. 237 (2002); Neal Devins and Louis Fisher, Judicial Exclusivity and Political Instability, 84 *VA. L. REV*. 83 (1998).

[39] See, e.g., *Arizona State Legis. v. Arizona Indep. Redistricting Commn.*, 135 S. Ct. 2652, 2697–99 (2015) (Thomas, J., dissenting) ("These sentiments are difficult to accept. The conduct of the Court in so many other cases reveals a different attitude toward the States in general and ballot initiatives in particular. Just last week, in the antithesis of deference to state lawmaking through direct democracy, the Court cast aside state laws across the country—many of which were enacted through ballot initiative—that reflected the traditional definition of marriage ... This Court's tradition of disdain for state ballot initiatives goes back quite a while. Two decades ago, it held unconstitutional an Arkansas ballot initiative imposing term limits on that State's Members of Congress, finding 'little significance' in the fact that such term limits were adopted by popular referendum ... One year later, it held unconstitutional a ballot initiative that would have prevented the enactment of laws under which 'homosexual, lesbian or bisexual orientation, conduct, practices or relationships [would] constitute or otherwise be the basis of ... any minority status, quota preferences, protected status or claim of discrimination.' ... The Court neither gave deference to state lawmaking nor said anything about the virtues of direct democracy. It instead declared that the result of the ballot initiative was an aberration—that '[i]t is not within our constitutional tradition to enact laws of this sort.' But if 'constitutional tradition' is the measuring stick, then it is hard to understand how the Court condones a redistricting practice that was unheard of for nearly 200 years after the ratification of the Constitution and that conflicts with the express constitutional command that election laws 'be prescribed in each State by the Legislature thereof,' Art. I, § 4. Id." (citations omitted)).

[40] See Pamela S. Karlan and Daniel R. Ortiz, Constitutional Elitism—Some Skepticism About Dogmatic Assertions, 30 *McGeorge L. Rev*. 117 (1998), available https://scholarlycommons.pacific.edu/mlr/vol30/iss1/9; Lawrence Baum and Neal Devins, Why the Supreme Court Cares About Elites, Not the American People (2010). Faculty Publications 1116, available https://scholarship.law.wm.edu/facpubs/1116; David Chang, A Critique

"the larger the political community, the smaller will the proportion of the governing minority to the governed majority be, and the more difficult will it be for the majority to organize for reaction against the minority ... ruling minorities are usually so constituted that the individuals who make them up are distinguished from the mass of the governed by qualities that give them a certain material, intellectual or even moral superiority."[41] LAPP, in conjunction with MEF enables the disaggregation of the politicized interests and ideological components of the Court's power that render it a policymaking institution that vies for power in the tripartite government structure of American law, society, and politics.[42] As noted by Bentley, the

> Supreme Court will effectively use whichever line of reasoning it wishes, to state and explain to the country the decision which it will actually render on lines which, although passing through reasoning, are reasoning's masters, not its servants. The most perfect of logical machines, set to the Constitution and to all the precedents, would have pathways through it which would deliver simultaneous contradictory judgments on the same point without the slightest shock to its mechanism. Compared with the multiform irregularities of the pressure of the interest groups in a highly complex society, the finest legal logic is but a trivial fly-by-night, and the very essence of unreliability.[43]

The common factor, ordering principle, nexus that links the Court to the other political branches is elitist control and management of government and governance. Staunch advocates and apologists of the elitist nature of Court power that are unwilling to consider how its elitist nature actively and substantially affects and effects challenges to representation and democracy are not constructive. Such analyses obscure the deep structural effects, consequences, impact on the more fundamental question of what exactly is the point of claiming to possess representative and

of Judicial Supremacy, 36 *Vill. L. Rev.* 281 (1991), available https://digitalcommons.law.villanova.edu/vlr/vol36/iss2/1.

[41] See Mosca, supra note 11 at 53.

[42] See Marvin L. Astrada, The Nature of the Judicial Process: A Complex Systems Analysis of Checks & Balances & Separation of Powers in the Present Political Context, 21 *Rich. Pub. Int. L. Rev.* 263 (2017), available https://scholarship.richmond.edu/pilr/vol21/iss3/4.

[43] Bentley, supra note 8 at 394.

democratic politics, and the purpose of government, if elite checks on the peoples are the norm.[44] The Court itself has noted that, "if We The Court conclude that They The People's answers to a problem are silly, we are free to 'interven[e]' ... but if we too are uncertain of the right answer, or merely think the States may be on to something, we [the Court] can loosen the leash."[45]

If government is comprised of identarian-informed interest and activity, and groups carry out activity on the larger legal and political stages, and if interests are attached to groups via identity and the politics of identity, then it seems incumbent upon us to analyze elitism and representational politics from a structural perspective. Indeed, politicized identity may have an adverse effect on the representativeness of politics, and on the overarching democratic political system as a whole.[46] Identity is not

[44] *United States v. Morrison*, 529 U.S. 598, 616 (2000) ("ever since Marbury this Court has remained the ultimate expositor of the constitutional text."). "Under the leadership of Jefferson and Madison, Republicans championed an expansive ideal of popular authority, insisting on the people's right to control their representatives at all times and on all issues. Hamilton's Federalists, in contrast, became progressively more conservative and anti-populist, defending a philosophy that acknowledged the political power of ordinary citizens on election days but called upon them between elections to defer passively and unquestioningly to 'constituted authorities."' Larry D. Kramer, Marbury and the Retreat from Judicial Supremacy, 605 *Constitutional Commentary* 205–30 (2003), available https://scholarship.law.umn.edu/concomm/605.

[45] *McDonald v. City of Chicago*, 561 U.S. 742, 803 (2010).

[46] "If the people are the sovereign from which all power originates, then why should their expression of will not carry more weight than the legislature's crude effort to approximate it? If the root difficulty of judicial review is its counter-majoritarian nature, why does the argument for judicial intervention not abate as it becomes clearer what the majority prefers?" Julian N. Eule, Judicial Review of Direct Democracy, 99 *YALE L.J.* 1503, 1506 (1990). See also Kramer, "Marbury," supra note 44 at 217. "Federalism was from the first a rejection of the unruly style of popular politics that Revolutionary leaders had practiced against England in the 1760s. It was an effort to preserve the tradition of deference that, in the eyes of the elite, was essential to keep republican politics from spinning out of control. Somewhat muted in the 1780s, this mild conservatism became increasingly pronounced as time passed. Federalists never wanted to anoint a King or create a hereditary aristocracy, as Republicans sometimes charged. But the 'democracy' they believed in was, as Gordon Wood has put it, 'a patrician-led classical democracy in which virtue exemplified in government will diffuse its salutary influence through[out] the society.' Federalists witnessed the effects of the Revolution, observed their leadership being challenged by farmers, mechanics, and shopkeepers, and did not like what they saw." Id.

static. The actual populace, the peoples—as opposed to the People—is not subject to any one elite subgroup's ownership as far as content, application, and articulation of interests. Meaning, as the Court notes in the case of citizenship, nationality, and the Eighth Amendment, is fluid, ever-changing, and subject to evolving standards of comprehension and actuality.[47] Yet, there seems to be an underlying continuity in American politics that is reflected in MEF and LAPP, viz., that the Court functions as a powerful check on popular or democratic government, and does so, in part through a monopoly over what constitutes the People under the fundamental law.[48]

To view the question of the elitist nature of the Court and its role in government employing LAPP, and to view it within the structural context of law as activity, groups, interest, and identity vis-à-vis representative government, is to go beyond Court pronouncements legitimating its power,[49] or other status-quo rationalizations for accepting, lauding, or justifying the nonrepresentative, elitist components, and character of the Court. Apologists, passive acceptance, as well as advocates for embracing the elitist nature of the Court[50] distort and simplify Court power. The polity is, in short, subject to the Court's pronouncements when it exercises review and supremacy.[51] How the Court interprets the People thus

[47] *Trop v. Dulles*, 356 U.S. 86, 100–101 (1958). The Court recognized in [*Weems v. United States*, 217 U.S. 349,] that the words of the Amendment are not precise, and that their scope is not static. The Amendment must draw its meaning from the evolving standards of decency that mark the progress of a maturing society." Id.

[48] See Frederick Schauer, The Questions of Authority, 81 *GEO. L.J.* 95 (1992).

[49] See, e.g., *Bd. of Trs. of Univ. of Ala. v. Garrett*, 531 U.S. 356 (2001); *Kimel v. Fla. Bd. of Regents*, 528 U.S. 62 (2000); *United States v. Morrison*, 529 U.S. 598 (2000); *Dickerson v. United States*, 530 U.S. 428 (2000); *City of Boerne v. Flores*, 521 U.S. 507 (1997); *Cooper v. Aaron*, 358 U.S. 1 (1958).

[50] See Frank I. Michelman, Living with Judicial Supremacy, 38 *Wake Forest L. Rev.* 579 (2003); L.A. Powe, Jr., The Politics of American Judicial Review: Reflections on the Marshall, Warren, and Rehnquist Courts, 38 *Wake Forest L. Rev.* 697 (2003); Saikrishna B. Prakash and John C. Yoo, The Origins of Judicial Review, 70 *U. Chi. L. Rev.* 887 (2003); Robert A. Schapiro, Judicial Deference and Interpretive Coordinacy in State and Federal Constitutional Law, 85 *Cornell L. Rev.* 656 (2000); Keith E. Whittington, Extrajudicial Constitutional Interpretation: Three Objections and Responses, 80 *N.C. L. Rev.* 773 (2002); Brian M. Feldman, Note, Evaluating Public Endorsement of the Weak and Strong Forms of Judicial Supremacy, 89 *VA. L. Rev.* 979 (2003).

[51] See Robert L. Clinton, Democracy, the Supreme Court, and Our Two Constitutions, 8 *Faulkner L. Rev.* 4–5 (2016). "Constitutional judicial review is simply the authority of

has a direct impact on the character and content of operative terms such as *citizen*, *polity*, *law*, *common good*, *general welfare*, and *governance*. "'A body politic ... is a social compact by which the whole people covenants with each citizen, and each citizen with the whole people, that all shall be governed by certain laws for the common good.'"[52] Court discourse in the form of opinions creates a counter-discourse to that of the other two branches of government that are, to some degree, accountable to the people. "How many people today live in a language that is not their own? Or no longer, or not yet, even know their own and know poorly the major language that they are forced to serve?"[53] Herein lies a fundamental aspect of Court power, i.e., its conceptual discourse forms the firmament of legal thought vis-à-vis constitutional legibility.[54] The Court, for instance, has declared: "[I]n *the name of the American people*; in this court, every state in the union is represented; we are constituted by the voice of the union, and when decisions take place, which nothing but a

a court (any court) to disregard an otherwise applicable law in the decision of a particular case, when it determines that law to be incompatible with an applicable constitutional provision. As such, judicial review is a normal part of the judicial function and is a power possessed by any court with authority to apply constitutional law in the decision of cases and controversies. On the other hand, federal judicial supremacy, as it is presently understood, refers to the power of federal courts-the Supreme Court in particular-to issue binding, conclusive proclamations on the meaning of all provisions in the United States Constitution. To put the matter in the language of modem political correctness, judicial review is 'inclusive' (all courts have it), while judicial supremacy is 'exclusive' (only the Supreme Court has it in the last analysis)." Id.

[52] *Munn v. Illinois*, 94 U.S. 113, 124 (1876).

[53] Gilles Deleuze and Felix Guattari, "Kafka: Toward a Minor Literature" 1598–1601, 1601 (trans. Dana Poland in The Norton Anthology of Theory & Criticism, eds. Vincent B. Leitch, et al., 2001).

[54] See Mosca, supra note 11 at 153–54."[Some] of the main considerations that most seriously undermine the foundations on which universal suffrage as an intellectual edifice rests. We deem it sufficient for our purposes here to demonstrate that the assumption that the elected official is the mouthpiece of the majority of his electors is as a rule not consistent with the facts ... What happens in other forms of government namely, that an organized minority imposes its will on the disorganized majority happens also and to perfection, whatever the appearances to the contrary, under the representative system. When we say that the voters 'choose' their representative, we are using a language that is very inexact ... In elections, as in all other manifestations of social life, those who have the will and, especially, the moral, intellectual and material means to force their will upon others take the lead over the others and command them." Id.

spirit to give ground and harmonize can reconcile, ours is the superior claim upon the comity of the state tribunals."[55]

Configurations of power that propagate a "true" homogenizing discourse must be critically examined, and the discourse propagated subjected to disaggregation, since the means of power that prevail provide the capacity to manage as well as manufacture mechanisms of control, e.g., the fundamental law. The fundamental law generates truth, knowledge, power, and right (correctness).[56] The polymorphous capacity of language, discourse, the primary vehicle through which the Court exercises its power,[57] has profound consequences for how classification, definition, and/or usage of concepts will manifest themselves in actuality. The fact that "people experience their present naively, as it were without being able to form an estimate of its contents,"[58] requires that those who propagate knowledge and truth be subjected to a "strict scrutiny standard." As C. Wright Mills, observes, "much power today is successfully employed without the sanction of the reason or the conscience of the obedient."[59] Nothing, therefore, "ought to keep us from directing our

[55] *Martin v. Hunter's Lessee*, 14 U.S. 304, 364–65 (1816).

[56] See Michel Foucault, Power/Knowledge: Selected Interviews and Other Writings, 1972–1977, ed. Colin Gordon (1980).

[57] See Federalist no. 78 (Hamilton), Avalon Project, Yale University, available https://avalon.law.yale.edu/18th_century/fed78.asp. "Whoever attentively considers the different departments of power must perceive, that, in a government in which they are separated from each other, the judiciary, from the nature of its functions, will always be the least dangerous to the political rights of the Constitution; because it will be least in a capacity to annoy or injure them. The Executive not only dispenses the honors, but holds the sword of the community. The legislature not only commands the purse, but prescribes the rules by which the duties and rights of every citizen are to be regulated. The judiciary, on the contrary, has no influence over either the sword or the purse; no direction either of the strength or of the wealth of the society; and can take no active resolution whatever. It may truly be said to have neither FORCE nor WILL, but merely judgment; and must ultimately depend upon the aid of the executive arm even for the efficacy of its judgments. This simple view of the matter suggests several important consequences. It proves incontestably, that the judiciary is beyond comparison the weakest of the three departments of power1; that it can never attack with success either of the other two; and that all possible care is requisite to enable it to defend itself against their attacks. It equally proves, that though individual oppression may now and then proceed from the courts of justice, the general liberty of the people can never be endangered from that quarter." Id.

[58] Sigmund Freud, The Future of an Illusion 8 (intro. Peter Gay, ed. & trans. James Strachy, 1961).

[59] C. Wright Mills, The Sociological Imagination, Afterword Todd Gitlin (1959) 41.

observation to our own selves or from applying our thought to criticism itself."[60]

Concepts, discourse, can be analogized to abstract nets that are placed over a particular subject. That is,

> different nets correspond to different systems for describing the world. Mechanics determines one form of description of the world by saying that all propositions used in the description of the world must be obtained in a given way from a given set of propositions—the axiom of mechanics. It thus supplies the bricks for building the edifice of [knowledge], and it says, 'Any building that you want to erect, whatever it may be, must somehow be constructed with these bricks, and these alone.'[61]

Court opinions constitute a lattice, a conceptual repository, of analytic 'bricks,' that profoundly impact the character and content of democratic politics and the rule of law.[62] "This court has always acted up to the letter and spirit of the Constitution, and it is a subject of rejoicing that its opinions have found their way into the hearts of the people, and become guides of action."[63] The Court thinks that the peoples should rejoice, embrace the Court with its heart, the proposition that the Court will

[60] Freud, supra note 58 at 43. See also Roderick M. Hills, Jr., Are Judges Really More Principled Than Voters? 37 *U.S.F. L. Rev.* 37 (2002).

[61] Ludwig Wittgenstein, Tractatus Logico-Philosophicus 82 (trans. D.F. Pears and B.F. McGuiness, 1975). In the case of the Founding and Federalist thought, "Federalists recognized that they needed permission to rule, permission that had to be sought in free republican elections. But once this permission had been granted, ordinary citizens were supposed to lose their political agency. '[T]he sovereignty of the people is delegated to those whom they have freely appointed to administer [the] constitution, and by them alone can be rightly exercised, save at the stated period of election, when the sovereignty is again at the disposal of the whole people.' Between elections, the people needed only to listen and to obey. Unity, 'respectability,' order, and, above all, reverence for constituted authorities were the hallmarks Federalists looked for in a well-functioning political system." Kramer, "Marbury," supra note 44 at 217–18.

[62] "'The [Supreme Court] by declaring every local or internal law of Congress constitutional, would extend its own jurisdiction; a limitation of which, attended with a power to extend it without control, by a supreme power over the state courts, would be no limitation at all; since the power of supremacy would destroy the co-ordinate right of construing the constitution, in which resides the power of enforcing the limitation. The jurisdiction, limited by its own will, is an unlimited jurisdiction.'" Joseph L. Call, Judicial Review vs. Judicial Supremacy, 62 *Dick. L. Rev.* 71, 73 (1957).

[63] *State v. Baltimore & O.R. Co.*, 44 U.S. 534, 546 (1845)

provide the definitive legal, political, moral, and sociocultural guideposts for the correct ordering of society. Questions pertaining to a nondemocratic life-tenured Court, the Court as agent of government, and the real and substantive consequences of having such a medium of government and governance for facilitating representative government caution against uncritically subscribing to the Court's admonition.

The Court's power is thus not divorced from the present existential crisis facing the American polity. If representation, diversity, equity, equality, accountability, fairness, and attenuation of privilege are being actively sought out in the present and are rallying cries for substantive change for the future, then the Court's power and place in the overarching governmental structure requires critical examination. Consider, for example, the doctrine of Qualified Immunity established wholly by Court opinions, which has been used to shield police officers from lawsuits. Qualified immunity

> has emerged as one of the most significant and problematic defenses to claims of civil rights violations. Its development in the Supreme Court has been marked by ad hoc decision-making, conflicting rationales, and a high degree of doctrinal manipulation. Today, it stands as a legal principle defined primarily by the Court's own policy judgment that an individual's right to compensation for constitutional violations and the deterrence of unconstitutional conduct should be subordinated to the governmental interest in effective and vigorous execution of governmental policies and programs. Given the broad barriers to damage actions erected by the Court in its construction of the immunity doctrine, one would expect strong constitutional or statutory support for such a defense. The Constitution, however, provides no basis for qualified immunity, and, on its face, the language of § 1983 'admits of no immunities.'[64]

The nature, purpose, and disposition of American government, and the modalities employed to govern, must therefore be subject to scrutiny.[65]

[64] David Rudovsky, The Qualified Immunity Doctrine in the Supreme Court: Judicial Activism & the Restriction of Constitutional Rights (1989). Faculty Scholarship at Penn Law. 1507, available https://scholarship.law.upenn.edu/faculty_scholarship/1507.

[65] See H. Jefferson Powell, Enslaved to Judicial Supremacy? 106 *HARV. L. REV*. 1197, 1197 (1993) ("[f]or most of our history, most Americans have seen the Supreme Court as the ultimate interpreter of the Constitution, entitled (this side of an amendment) to impose its understanding of the Constitution on the states, the other branches of the federal government, and the people"). See also *U.S. v. California*, 332 U.S. 19 (1946).

In the case of Court power, the People is one such (elitist) modality. As noted by Justice Stone, "While unconstitutional exercise of power by the executive and legislative branches of the government is subject to judicial restraint, the only check on our exercise of power is our own sense of self-restraint."[66]

Disaggregating the People enables one to effectively question the uniquely elitist character of the Court's power, and how it ostensibly seems to fit quite seamlessly into a democratic political system governed by representation and ROL. The elitist and unrepresentative nature of *how* the Court exercises its power—not the actual outcomes of cases—sheds light on the inherent tensions that inform the present legal and political process premised on democratic representation. The elite underpinnings of constitutional order, and the Court's role as steward for its preservation, perpetuation, and integrity, directly impact the actual peoples in every facet of its being.[67] Constitutional reality, and its limitations, in

As Call, supra note 62 at 81–83 n. 41, observes about the foregoing case: "This decision of the Supreme Court quieted title of the United States against the State of California in fee simple for possession of all rights and powers over the lands and minerals and other things of value underlying the Pacific Ocean and lying seaward of the ordinary low water mark for 3 nautical miles is based on the premise that '. . . the Federal Government rather than the State has paramount rights in their power over that belt, and incident to which is full dominion over the resources of the soil under that water, including oil.' The doctrine of 'paramount rights' is not to be found in any of the delegations of power given by the people or the States to the Federal government in the United States Constitution, nor can it be implied therefrom. The only effect that can be given to this decision is to read sovereignty and omnipotent power into the Federal Government." Id.

[66] *U.S. v. Butler*, 297 U.S. 1, 78 (1936).

[67] "By exercising the sole power to interpret its own authority as well as the authority of the Congress, the President, and the people, the Supreme Court has become absolute in its nature. As the power to interpret includes the power to change, it of course follows that the court is not only the guardian, but the master, of the Constitution. By such stewardship the sovereignty, vested constitutionally in the people, has now been absorbed by the court, and by such conversion it stands possessed as the ultimate sovereignty in the United States rather than the people themselves being and possessing the sovereign power." Call, supra note 62 at 83. Mosca notes that, "[I]n all the countries that have adopted universal suffrage more or less recently, the educated and well-to-do classes have maintained their rule under its aegis, though their influence has been tempered more or less by the influence of the petty bourgeoisie and of representatives of the interests of certain groups ... Democratic institutions may be able to endure for some time yet if, in virtue of them, a certain equilibrium between the various elements in the ruling class can be maintained, if our apparent democracy is not fatally carried away by logic, its worst enemy, and by the appetites of the lower classes and their leaders, and if it does

particular, depend, in part, on the philosophy of law employed by the Justices, and how each Justice perceives who or what constitutes the sovereign People.

> The answer at first may seem to be self-evident. The United States is a nation. The People of the United States is the American people … There are fifty states, but as Justice Black remarked, it is a simple 'fact that the States of the Union constitute a nation.' If we are one nation, are we not also one people? The question is not so open-and-closed, and the ultimate answer is not so simple. Indeed, the debate over the identity of the People still rages … the concept of popular sovereignty distinguishes between the exercise of power through the branches of government and the fundamental, arbitrary power held by the sovereign people … [Conceptually, we can divide debate] into two broad camps: nationalists and state-populists. Adherents of the former insist that the People—and the only existing people—is a national people. Those in the latter camp maintain that the several state peoples not only existed before the Constitution, but also survived ratification.[68]

The primary means by which the Court communicates its word, pronouncements, is through the medium of constitutional interpretation as embodied in Court opinions. This is how the Court speaks to or more accurately at the People, while concomitantly infusing the People with constitutionality. The nexus betwixt MEF and LAPP in the form of activity, groups, interests, and politics can be observed in Court opinions. Opinions provide a formal transcript of elite jurists explicating the law—permutations to include majority, plurality, concurring, individual, seriatim, and dissenting opinions—and articulating the fundamental law for the entire polity. Thus, opinions provide case studies that, when viewed systemically, provide insight into the overarching relationship between law, activity, groups, interests, and representative government.[69]

not attempt to become *real democracy by combining political equality with economic and cultural equality*" (emphasis added). Mosca, supra note 11 at 335.

[68] Andrew G. I. Kilberg, We the People: The Original Meaning of Popular Sovereignty, 100 *Va. L. Rev.* 1061, 1061–62 (2014).

[69] "Like the character of an individual, the legitimacy of the Court must be earned over time. So, indeed, must be the character of a Nation of people who aspire to live according to the rule of law. Their belief in themselves as such a people is not readily separable from their understanding of the Court invested with the authority to decide their constitutional cases and speak before all others for their constitutional ideals. If the

"It is always a matter of direct observation and of nothing else to show what law groups can be analyzed out of the mass."[70] Unanimous, majority, plurality, concurring, dissenting, and individual opinions of the Justices thus provide a working basis for critical analysis. It is important to note that while Court opinions provide insight into the nexus, nonetheless they do not necessarily provide a coherent basis upon which to ascertain and predict outcomes; "from the point of view of law as system is that complexes of groups, working together through the government, combine their pressures. There is nothing absolute about the combination. It doesn't conform to any theory, and even the best theory only poorly conforms to it. But where we have it, we have it; and at certain transition stages between adjustments, it seems to stand out as an independent factor."[71]

Constitutional law is by its nature an elitist construct, discourse, and to say that the make-up of the Court, its disconnectedness from the lives of most Americans, and its sweeping and final pronouncements on the fundamental law (wherein nine people decide the character and content of the American legal context for 330 million people) should give us pause, irrespective of one's ideological or political predispositions.[72] Analyzing the discourse of nondemocratic elite jurists that construct the fundamental law facilitates the "fullest and richest statement of the law [ ] in terms of the group activity tending to spread itself, with allowance for the

Court's legitimacy should be undermined, then, so would the country be in its very ability to see itself through its constitutional ideals. The Court's concern with legitimacy is not for the sake of the Court, but for the sake of the Nation to which it is responsible." *Planned Parenthood of S.E. Pennsylvania v. Casey*, 505 U.S. 833, 868 (1992).

[70] Bentley, supra note 8 at 287.

[71] Id.

[72] See Karlan, supra note 40 at 121. "[T]he charge of educational elitism is trivially true in one sense. Constitutional law does represent the work product of highly educated people. The judges, attorneys, and law clerks who most deeply shape constitutional law have received more schooling than most people. And, as a group, the Founders were certainly highly educated. That much is uncontroversial. As before, then, the more interesting question is a comparative one: are constitutional law's shapers more educated and more elite than the people who shape politics? Again, we're agnostic. The political elite is itself well-educated and the people who directly shape the largest body of our law-regulatory law-are certainly well-educated too. If it has any bite, the charge of educational elitism must mean that the educated people who shape constitutional law are more out of touch with the common person than are the educated people who shape other types of law. Is that true?" Id.

differences of technique in the governing organ through which it functions."[73] Hence, the types of opinions, pronouncements, that emanate from the Court provide a comprehensive view of the Court's power and impact on the peoples and democratic representative politics. The Court itself has acknowledged the somewhat reductionist or nonuniformity of its mandates, interpretation, and implementation based on the People as a cardinal ordering concept. "For instance, the Constitution provides that 'no person' shall be deprived of liberty without due process of law. And yet, as we know, whole generations of people in this land—as many as four millions of them at one time—people described in the Constitution by this same word, 'persons,' have been till lately deprived of liberty ever since the adoption of the Constitution, without any process of law whatever."[74]

Lastly, whether or not the Court has done "good" through individual rulings does not automatically legitimate an (nondemocratic, nonrepresentative) elitist ratiocination for the Court's power of review and supremacy.[75] It is the dynamics, character, content, and impact of the

[73] Bentley, supra note 8 at 291.

[74] *Ex parte Milligan*, 71 U.S. 2, 103 (1866).

[75] Indeed, while it can be forcibly argued that the Court has done "good," it can also be forcibly argued that the Court has done "not so good" when imposing its pronouncements on the polity (noting that "good" is a subjective and relative term that hinges on one's political, ideological, and overarching worldview). "Some decisions have empowered women, helped protect the environment, or guaranteed a person's right to expression. Others have strengthened racist laws, enabled forced sterilization, and allowed unequal schooling." James Pasley, "Landmark Supreme Court Cases That Changed American Life as We Knew It," Business Insider, August 29, 2019, available https://www.businessinsider.com/landmark-us-supreme-court-cases-2019-8. See, e.g., *Dred Scott v. Sandford*, 60 U.S. 393 (1857) (Under Fifth Amendment, slaves are property, and law that deprives a slave-owner of property unconstitutional); Plessy v. Ferguson, 163 U.S. 537 (1896) ("separate but equal" accommodations based on race does not violate the 14th Amendment); *Lochner v. New York*, 98 U.S. 45 (1905) (wherein limits on working time violate the Fourteenth Amendment and liberty to contract); *Abrams v. United States*, 250 U.S. 616 (1919) (willfully publishing 'disloyal' language that presents a "clear and present danger" about the government is not protected by the First Amendment); *Buck v. Bell*, 274 U.S. 207 (1927) ("We have seen more than once that the public welfare may call upon the best citizens for their lives. It would be strange if it could not call upon those who already sap the strength of the State for these lesser sacrifices, often not felt to be such by those concerned, in order to prevent our being swamped with incompetence. It is better for all the world, if instead of waiting to execute degenerate offspring for crime, or let them starve for their imbecility, society can prevent those who are manifestly unfit from breeding their kind. The principle that sustains compulsory vaccination is broad enough

Court's power that are the focus of critical inquiry. To brush off this operative and fundamental fact as trivial or uninteresting is to reify the elitist enterprise of control and management of law, society, and politics that is in line with a technical, procedural (as opposed to substantive) perception of representation and democracy.[76] "In practice, therefore, the representative system results not at all in government by the majority; it results in the participation of a certain number of social values in the guidance of the state."[77] The Court, in the name of the People, thus exercises substantial power in positing what constitutes a citizen, civic participation, rights, obligations, protections, and access to the mechanisms of power to influence public policy via certain social values, norms, and practices it feels qualify or do not qualify for constitutional stature under the U.S. Constitution.[78]

to cover cutting Fallopian tubes ... Three generations of imbeciles are enough."); *San Antonio Independent School District v. Rodriguez*, 411 U.S. 1 (1973) (no constitutional right to an equal education); *Michael H. v Gerald D.*, 491 U.S. 110 (1989) (Biological father does not have a fundamental right to obtain parental rights, after a presumed father has been responsible for a child); *Citizens United v. FEC*, 558 U.S. 310 (2010) (corporate contributions are deemed protected speech under First Amendment).

[76] "[E]very governing class tends to justify its actual exercise of power by resting it on some universal moral principle ... ruling classes do not justify their power exclusively by de facto possession of it, but try to find a moral and legal basis for it, representing it as the logical and necessary consequence of doctrines and beliefs that are generally recognized and accepted." Mosca, supra note 11 at 62, 70. See Jeremy Rabkin, Partisan in the Culture Wars, 30 *McGeorge L. Rev.* 105 (1998); *Romer v. Evans*, 517 U.S. 620, 636–53 (1996) (Scalia, J., dissenting) (the Court acts as a participant in the "culture wars" that divide America and that "in these conflicts, the Court is a systematic partisan for one side").

[77] Mosca, supra note 11 at 155. See Jane Mansbridge, et al., The Place of Self-Interest and the Role of Power in Deliberative Democracy, *The Journal of Political Philosophy*, vol. 18, no. 1 (2010) 64–100; Christopher A. Cooper, Anthony J. Nownes and Steven Roberts, *State & Local Government Review*, vol. 37, no. 3 (2005) 206–16; Abraham Zaleznik, Power and Politics in Organizational Life, *Harvard Business Review*, May 1970, available https://hbr.org/1970/05/power-and-politics-in-organizational-life.

[78] *Ableman v. Booth*, 62 U.S. 506, 517 (1858) (establishing that a federal court judgment in a criminal case was not subject to review by a state court.) "The Constitution was not formed merely to guard the States against danger from foreign nations, but mainly to secure union and harmony at home ... the supremacy thus conferred on this Government could not peacefully be maintained unless it was clothed with judicial power equally paramount in authority to carry it into execution."). Id.

CHAPTER 3

Step 3: The People as Political, Discursive and Legal Construct

Abstract A primary mechanism by which Court power can be critically assessed is through analysis of the People. On its face, the People seems to be quite direct as far as what it signifies. Yet upon closer inspection, this is not the case. The People and the people are distinct states of affairs. The Court has acknowledged that the People is a term of art, and it has provided differential interpolations of this "term of art" in its jurisprudence. The People, as opposed to the actual people that constitute the American populace, can be viewed as an act of imagination. The People, as an ideological and political construct, has been operative since before the founding. The People, in actuality is a complex legal and political construct—one that provides a primary basis for legitimizing the exercise of the Supreme Court's power. The Court has provided selective and, at times, seemingly contentious or differential notions of what the People are exactly within the fundamental law.

Keywords The people · The People · Fundamental law · Policy · Constitutional discourse

M. L. Astrada, *Law, Society & Politics*,
https://doi.org/10.1007/978-3-030-66714-6_3

A primary mechanism by which Court power can be critically assessed is through analysis of the People.[1] On its face, the People seems to be quite direct as far as what it signifies. The "Preamble declares who is enacting this Constitution—the people of 'the United States.' The document is the collective enactment of all U.S. citizens. The Constitution is 'owned' (so to speak) by the people, not by the government or any branch thereof. We the People are the stewards of the U.S. Constitution and remain ultimately responsible for its continued existence and its faithful interpretation."[2] Yet upon closer inspection, this is not the case.[3] The People and the people are distinct states of affairs. At base, "there is a national people, but it coexists with the sovereign state peoples. Furthermore, the national people must be interpreted through a lens of state peoples—the People is national in scope and importance, but it is defined in reference to the state peoples."[4] The Court, however, has emphatically

[1] This discussion draws from Marvin L. Astrada and Scott B. Astrada, Enemy at the Gates: The Consequential Effects of Securitizing Immigration, *Global Security and Intelligence Studies*, vol. 3, no. 2 (Fall/Winter 2018) 36–42.

[2] Erwin Chemerinsky and Michael Stokes Paulsen, "Common Interpretation: The Preamble," The National Constitution Center, available https://constitutioncenter.org/interactive-constitution/interpretation/preamble-ic/interps/37. Yet, "In the Preamble and in the Constitution itself ... the term 'people' is found only twice, plus seven times in the amendments; in the Constitution there is no significant current use of 'person' (although five pre-amendment uses may be referred to), while in the amendments proper there is a maximum use of only six such instances; and, finally, in the entirety of the Preamble, Constitution, and amendments, the maximum use of 'people' and 'persons' is therefore found in 15 instances. For a 'government of the people, by the people, for the people,' it seems almost sacrilegious that our fundamental document contains this term only twice, and only nine times if the subsequent amendments are added; and even if 'persons' is thrown in, the significant total rises only to a maximum of 15." Morris D. Forkosch, Who are the "People" in the Preamble to the Constitution, 19 Case W. Res. L. Rev. 644, 649 (1968), available https://scholarlycommons.law.case.edu/caselrev/vol19/iss3/8.

[3] See, e.g., Edmund Randolph, quoted in Legislative & Documentary History of the Bank of the United States by Mathew St. Clair Clarke (2017) 88. The "Preamble[,] if it be operative is a full constitution of itself, and the body of the constitution is useless; but that it is declarative only of the views of the convention, which they supposed would be best fulfilled by the powers delineated; and that such is the legitimate nature of preambles," Id.

[4] Andrew G. I. Kilberg, We the People: The Original Meaning of Popular Sovereignty, 100 *Va. L. Rev.* 1061, 1064 (2014).

declared that, "[f]or all the great purposes for which the Federal government was formed, we are one people, with one common country."[5] Yet, it has also acknowledged that the People is a term of art employed in select parts of the Constitution,[6] and it has provided differential interpretations of this "term of art" in its jurisprudence.[7] The Court has also acknowledged that the interpretive enterprise is quite vulnerable to the Court imposing its version or view of the parameters and content of "correct" legal process and resultant policy spaces. "Under the guise of interpreting the Constitution we must take care that we do not import into the discussion our own personal views of what would be wise, just, and fitting rules of government to be adopted by a free people, and confound them with constitutional limitations."[8] It is thus important to analyze and "explain the judiciary's competence to speak for the people"[9] due to the Court's confounding the People with the peoples.

The People, as opposed to the actual peoples that constitute the American populace, can be viewed as an act of imagination. The peoples "are certainly a collectivity, but what kind of collectivity are they? Are they a folk, nation, or race? Are they those who belong to the place or territory? Are they members of the congregation of the civic culture or religion? Are they the citizens or electorate? Or are they an indefinite collection of persons or individuals, that is just a sum of the parts?"[10] The People, as analytic instrumentation, has been designed to dispense with the complexities immanent in the foregoing questions. It is an invention employed at the founding and in the Court's jurisprudence to bypass the very problematic exercise of elite authorities giving voice, meaning, and substance, to the peoples in the legal and political process. The People, as an ideological and political construct, has been operative since before the founding,

[5] *Shapiro v. Thompson*, 394 U.S. 618, 630 (1969). The People of These United States Constitute One Nation." *Crandall v. State of Nevada*, 73 U.S. 35, 43 (1867).

[6] *United States v. Verdugo-Urquidez*, 494 U.S. 259, 265 (1990).

[7] See Note, The Meaning(s) of "The People" in the Constitution, 126 *Harv. L. Rev.* 1078 (2013).

[8] *Twining v. State of N.J.*, 211 U.S. 78, 106–7 (1908).

[9] Jed Rubenfeld, Reading the Constitution As Spoken, 104 *Yale L.J.* 1119, 1121 (1995).

[10] Ralph D. Church, WE THE PEOPLE: Reflections on the Meaning of the 'People' in The Constitution of the United States of America, *Il Politico*, vol. 57, no. 2 (162) (Aprile-Giugno 1992) 260–61.

and has been employed by elites other than the Court. In Federalist no. 2, for instance, John Jay's exposition of the People is explicitly employed to argue for the primacy, inevitability, organic nature of unity, union, and a singular People that he classifies as American in arguing for the ratification of the Constitution:

> it would conduce more to the interest of the people of America that they should, to all general purposes, be one nation, under one federal government ... the prosperity of the people of America depend[s] on their continuing firmly united ... [there is] safety and happiness in union ... Providence has been pleased to give this one connected country to one united people—a people descended from the same ancestors, speaking the same language, professing the same religion, attached to the same principles of government, very similar in their manners and customs, and who, by their joint counsels, arms, and efforts, fighting side by side throughout a long and bloody war, have nobly established general liberty and independence. This country and this people seem to have been made for each other, and it appears as if it was the design of Providence, that an inheritance so proper and convenient for a band of brethren, united to each other by the strongest ties, should never be split into a number of unsocial, jealous, and alien sovereignties ... To all general purposes we have uniformly been one people each individual citizen everywhere enjoying the same national rights, privileges, and protection.[11]

This conception of the People, which Jay argues is the lodestar and substratum of the Constitution, is, in short, severely inaccurate, neglecting the multifarious communities and subcommunities of people (human beings) who were not considered fully human under law at the time of the founding era, such as African slaves, women, children, and men without property.[12] The origins of the people is far more complicated. After putting forth a Declaration of Independence, Americans apparently

> located sovereignty squarely in the people themselves ... 'In planning a government by representation, the people ought to provide against their own annihilation, ... [and] establish a regular and constitutional method

[11] Federalist no. 2 (John Jay), available https://avalon.law.yale.edu/18th_century/fed02.asp.

[12] See Forkosch, supra note 2.

> of acting by and from themselves, without, or even in opposition to their representatives, if necessary' ... The revolutionaries 'groped awkwardly for some institutional representation of the people with which to justify the erection of new governments.'[13]

Furthermore, notions of person or peoplehood have been expanded by the Court to include nonhuman entities such as corporations in its construction of what constitute the People under law.[14]

The People, in actuality is a complex legal and political construct—one that provides a primary basis for legitimizing the exercise of the Supreme Court's power. The Court has provided nuanced and, at times, seemingly contentious or differential notions of what the People are exactly within the fundamental law.[15] Thus, the questions posed by Justice Wilson in 1793, that is, "'The PEOPLE of the United States' are the first personages introduced [in the Preamble]. Who were those people," and "'do the people of the United States form a Nation?'"[16] are as relevant today as they were in 1793. Indeed, the Court has ostensibly interpreted "the People" in a straightforward manner. The People are, in short, the wellspring of power and the ultimate authority in the constitutional order:

[13] Kilberg, supra note 4 at 1061, 1076.

[14] See, e.g., *Santa Clara County v. Southern Pac. R.R.*, 118 U.S. 394, 396 (1886).

[15] See *United States v. Verdugo-Urquidez*, 494 U.S. 259, 265 (1990) ("the people" protected by the Fourth Amendment, and by the First and Second Amendments, and to whom rights and powers are reserved in the Ninth and Tenth Amendments, refers to a class of persons who are part of a national community or who have otherwise developed sufficient connection with this country to be considered part of that community."); *U.S. ex rel. Turner v. Williams*, 194 U.S. 279, 291 (1904) ("No limits can be put by the courts upon the power of Congress to protect, by summary methods, the country from the advent of aliens whose race or habits render them undesirable as citizens, or to expel such if they have already found their way into our land, and unlawfully remain therein."); *Kwong Hai Chew v. Colding*, 344 U.S. 590, 589 (1953) ("Bill of Rights is a futile authority for an alien seeking admission for the first time to the United States, but once an alien lawfully enters and resides in this country, he becomes invested with the rights guaranteed by the Constitution to all people within our borders, including the rights protected by the First and Fifth Amendments and by the due process clause of the Fourteenth Amendment.")

[16] *Chisholm v. Georgia*, 2 U.S. 419, 453, 463 (1793). See *Jacobson v. Massachusetts*, 197 U.S. 11, 22 (1905) ("Although that Preamble indicates the general purposes for which the people ordained and established the Constitution, it has never been regarded as the source of any substantive power conferred on the Government of the United States or on any of its Departments.").

> [T]he Constitution itself is, in every real sense, a law—the lawmakers being the people themselves, in whom, under our system, all political power and sovereignty primarily resides, and through whom such power and sovereignty primarily speaks. It is by that law, and not otherwise, that the legislative, executive, and judicial agencies which it created exercise such political authority as they have been permitted to possess. The Constitution speaks for itself in terms so plain that to misunderstand their import is not rationally possible. 'We the people of the United States,' it says, 'do ordain and establish this Constitution' ... Ordain and establish! These are definite words of enactment, and, without more, would stamp what follows with the dignity and character of law.[17]

The Court has also stated that,

> [I]n our system, while sovereign powers are delegated to the agencies of government, sovereignty itself remains with the people, by whom and for whom all government exists and acts. And the law is the definition and limitation of power. It is, indeed, quite true that there must always be lodged somewhere, and in some person or body, the authority of final decision, and in many cases of mere administration, the responsibility is purely political, no appeal lying except to the ultimate tribunal of the public judgment, exercised either in the pressure of opinion or by means of the suffrage. But the fundamental rights to life, liberty, and the pursuit of happiness, considered as individual possessions, are secured by those maxims of constitutional law which are the monuments showing the victorious progress of the race in securing to men the blessings of civilization under the reign of just and equal laws.[18]

The Court has been consistent in claiming that, "The Constitution of the United States was made by, and for the protection of, the people of the United States,"[19] and that it "was ordained and established by the people of the United States for themselves, for their own government ... The people of the United States framed such a government for the United States as they supposed best adapted to their situation and best

[17] *Carter v. Carter Coal Co.*, 298 U.S. 238, 296 (1936).

[18] *Yick Wo v. Hopkins*, 118 U.S. 356, 370 (1886).

[19] *League v. De Young*, 52 U.S. 184, 203 (1851).

calculated to promote their interests."[20] Yet, how the Court construes the People, e.g., a nationalist construction vs. a States-based construction, in the fundamental law is independent of the actual physical people(s), the population itself, that are subject to the singular pronouncements of the Court. Court interpretations of the People are analytically distinct from the people that reside in the ambit of Court power, that is, the American population, which is distinct from the People as a product of Court power.[21]

A. The People & peoples: Interpretation of the Fundamental Law as an Exercise of Power

Values play a cardinal role in laying the foundation for structuring perception, thought, and judgment. Perceptions are the basis upon which thought manifests in the empirical realm, which lays the conceptual foundation for judgment. Judgment, the normative pronouncement as to what is right, true, good, necessary, finds empirical expression in law and policy. Judgment is shaped by a subject's ability to perceive, conceive, process, and rationalize data. Judgments, which are objects of thought, are products of perception. Perceptions, in turn, are underpinned by norms and values. Thus, the character and content of law and policy will be directly affected and effected by framing and analyzing the legal and political process from a *peoples* perspective because it constitutes a specific constellation of values—integrity, dignity, fairness, impartiality, and equity—which color thought and judgment. Perceptions are the initial building blocks that provide the conceptual scaffolding for policy content and spaces. Perceptions, thought, and (ultimately) judgments

[20] *Barron v. Mayor of Balt.*, 32 U.S. 243, 247 (1833) (superseded on other grounds by Constitutional Amendment, U.S. CONST. Amend. XIV). See also *Martin v. Hunter's Lessee*, 14 U.S. 304, 324–25 (1816); *McCulloch v. Maryland*, 17 U.S. 316, 402–3 (1819).

[21] See Elizabeth Anne Reese, Or to the People: Popular Sovereignty and the Power to Choose A Government, 39 *Cardozo L. Rev.* 2051, 2093 (2018) (Analyzing the complex dynamics and implications of various ways to define the "people," e.g., the people as an independent nationalist collective, as being a State-based and State-dependent concept, or as a distinct state of affairs located in the 10th Amendment).

influence and are influenced by law, and are "central to, the construction of citizen attitudes and understandings"[22] of policy problems and proposed solutions.

Judgment, whether in the form of a court opinion, a decision to charge a defendant or mitigate a sentence, or as a statute addressing the general welfare and public interest, is tied to the values that underpin and structure thought and practice. Consider, for instance, the notion that socioeconomic identity, informed by various values—such as the meaning and worth attached to class, racial, and ethnic identity signifiers—assumes a profound role in how defendants are perceived and ultimately processed. Law can either acknowledge and consider or disregard the sundry norms and values that tincture the administration of justice. Perception, thought, judgment, and operationalization of the criminal justice system has been affected by different constellations of norms and values via philosophical views of punishment.[23] Another example is what has been termed the "crime of identity," which is informed by racial/ethnic and socioeconomic status. This "crime" occurs when social identity is employed to ascertain the guilt or innocence of a defendant.[24] The relationship between perception, thought, and judgment thus has a direct impact on the legal process and the empirical manifestation of politics and socioeconomic and political actualities in policy spaces. For example, on a more general level of thought and analysis, Thomas Paine notes this phenomena when critically considering the relationship between society and government:

> Some writers have so confounded society with government, as to leave little or no distinction between them; whereas they are not only different,

[22] Mario L. Barnes, Empirical Methods and Critical Race Theory: A Discourse on Possibilities for a Hybrid Methodology, 2016 *Wis. L. Rev.* 443, 445 (2016).

[23] See Marvin L. Astrada, Reentry Philosophies, Approaches, and Challenges, 102 JUDICATURE32 (2018). "Competing notions of crime and punishment have shaped the administration of criminal justice in the United States ever since the Quakers established the Walnut Street Prison in 1773 in Philadelphia, creating the first penitentiary in the country. Since then, the form and substance of criminal punishment have evolved from penitence, to rehabilitation, to retribution. From the mid-1970s onward, public policy has emphasized punishment and retribution" Id.

[24] Devon Carbado, (E)racing the Fourth Amendment, 100 *MICH. L. REV.* 946, 962 (2002). See also Mario L. Barnes, Black Women's Stories and the Criminal Law: Restating the Power of Narrative, 39 UC DAVIS L. REV. 941 (2006). (exploring how social identity may directly inform how one is treated within the criminal justice system.)

> but have different origins. Society is produced by our wants, and government by our wickedness; the former promotes our happiness positively, by uniting our affections; the latter negatively, by restraining our vices. The one encourages intercourse, the other creates distinctions. The first is a patron, the last punisher. Society in every state is a blessing, but government, even in its best state, is but a necessary evil; in its worst state, an intolerable one; for when we suffer, or are exposed to the same miseries by a government, which we might expect in a country without government, our calamity is heightened by reflecting that we furnish the means by which we suffer.[25]

Paine's analysis distinguishing between society and government can be applied to the People and the *peoples*, wherein a "faction of The People ... are invested with the authority of" the *peoples*.[26] Each of the foregoing signifiers encompasses a different constellation of norms and values upon which perception, thought and judgment are effectuated.

When considering the role of the *peoples* in law and policy, and MEF as an overarching organizing notion for law and politics, it is imperative to consider how ideational variables such as values inform perceptions and thought, which, in turn, are the basis for adjudging policy. The *peoples* differs from the People in that the constellation of norms and values can be distinguished. The *peoples*, as a signifier for what animates and justifies authority and law, explicitly considers and incorporates the socioeconomic actualities that underpin the populace's interests. This enables genuine representation of the actual peoples by addressing the empirical conditions, e.g., penury and racial identity, that contextualize the peoples' socioeconomic realities. Doing so serves the peoples rather than converting them into a formal, corporate entity of the People—which is informed by the structural values of political, social, and economic order, government, authority, legitimacy, governance, and the maintenance and enhancement of elites' power.[27]

[25] Thomas Paine, Common Sense, in David A. Hollinger & Charles Capper, The American Intellectual Tradition, 7th ed., vol. 1 (2016) 140, 139–147.

[26] Walter Lippmann, Essays in the Public Philosophy (1955) 34.

[27] See Heinrich Best & John Higley (eds.), The Palgrave Handbook of Political Elites (2018). See also Isaac Kramnick, Introduction in James Madison, Alexander Hamilton & John Jay, The Federalist Papers (1987) 16.

The motives and purposes that inform law and directly impact policy spaces will change depending on which constellation of values—the People or the *peoples*—is employed. How each of these signifiers is perceived and conceived directly impacts the operationalization of authority, perceptions of public interest, and the interpretation of fundamental rights vis-à-vis policy in the context of democratic politics. The People, for example, encompasses the notion that the "mass cannot govern. The people, as Jefferson said, are not 'qualified to exercise themselves the Executive Department; but they are qualified to name the person who shall exercise it ... They are not qualified to legislate; with us therefore they only choose the legislators.'"[28] It is thus "necessary at the outset to reduce the ambiguity of the term 'the people.' For it has two different meanings, which it may be convenient to distinguish ... When we speak of popular sovereignty, we must know whether we are talking about The People, as voters [for example], or about The [p]eople, as a community of the entire living population, with their predecessors and successors."[29] Building on this distinction, we can then examine whether the *peoples* better reflects "the vital interests of the community"[30] within the context of the criminal justice system.

Walter Lippmann, in analyzing the philosophical bases of policy-making, points out that the People of the Preamble are not representative of the nation, the peoples, as a whole. The People is an instrumentation manufactured for ordering, managing, and legitimizing a constellation of government, authority, and power that is posited in the name of the peoples over whom power and control are exercised. The People can be viewed as a corporate entity that has roots in "natural aristocracy," wherein there is congruence betwixt the minority elite in power and the mass of the peoples.[31] The People, as a functional, formal, corporate entity that reflects the priorities of a ruling class[32] is thus informed by a distinct constellation of norms and values that do not necessarily reflect the actualities of the *peoples*, which can be viewed as an aggregate of individuals, communities, and subcommunities whose interests should

[28] Thomas Jefferson, quoted in Lippmann, supra note 26 at 14–15.

[29] Lippmann, supra note 26 at 31–32.

[30] Id. at 32.

[31] See Id. at 32–35.

[32] See Gaetano Mosca, The Ruling, Class, trans. Hannah D. Kahn (1939).

be represented in democratic government, governance, law, and policy. The *peoples* comprise "the stream of individuals, the connected generations of changing persons"[33] that gives rise to and justifies the People which, in turn, divests the people*s* of significant degrees of representation in the articulation of law and policy.

The People as reflected in the Preamble, Constitution, and the U.S. Supreme Court's interpretation of the Constitution, is therefore a "corporation, an entity, that is to say, which lives on while individuals come into it and go out of it."[34] The People is thus a corporate body that includes those that were, e.g., the Founding generation, those that are (in the present historical moment), and those that will be.[35] The People is macroscopic in application, and transcends the individual subcomponents that it relies upon for legitimacy, i.e., the actual peoples.

How does law and policy reflect the People or the *peoples* exactly?[36] How does each find empirical expression in the law? The question of who exactly constitutes the People or the *peoples* and how each does or does not manifest is one of power and privilege. In Federalist No. 10, Madison explicitly articulates the elitist (natural aristocracy) foundation for American government: governance to protect the opulent minority (via the People) from "the superior force of an interested and overbearing majority"[37] (the peoples). The minute subsection of the polity that possesses the ability to define—and associate itself as protector of—the People is correlated with elite sociocultural, political, and economic status.[38] Law

[33] Lippmann, supra note 26 at 35.

[34] Id. at 35.

[35] Id. at 36.

[36] Marvin L. Astrada, Visions of the Republic Symposium: The People: A Pre-Primer for Critically Reevaluating Representation & Court Power in the Present, 88 *Fordham L. R. Online* 166 (2019), available https://ir.lawnet.fordham.edu/flro/vol88/iss1/13.

[37] James Madison, The Federalist, no. 10, available https://avalon.law.yale.edu/18th_century/fed10.asp.

[38] The sentiment undergirding the desire for a second legislative chamber (U.S. Senate) during the founding era reflects the norms and values that inform the People: "most Americans were still convinced of the need for a chamber that would represent superior talent and wisdom, where the more contemplative and learned in the community could revise the more hasty actions of the people. In this sense many Americans were like Thomas Jefferson in his belief both in the integrity and good sense of the common man, and in the existence of a 'natural aristocracy,' as he called it ..." Kramnick, supra note 27 at 21.

and public policy thus reflect the politics that attaches to defining what exactly constitutes the American P/people(s).[39] The *peoples*, on the other hand, signifies the actual subjects that constitute the physical population, to include sociocultural, political, and economic complexity that informs their interests. The *peoples* considers the substantive content of those subjects for whom authority speaks when articulating and enunciating law and policy.

On its face, the People may seem a straightforward signifier. It refers to the American People. Yet, the People is not necessarily indicative of the actual peoples. As noted earlier, the "Preamble declares who is enacting this Constitution—the people of 'the United States.' The document is the collective enactment of all U.S. citizens. The Constitution is 'owned' ... by the people, not by the government or any branch thereof. We the People are the stewards of the U.S. Constitution and remain ultimately responsible for its continued existence and its faithful interpretation."[40] Yet, upon closer inspection, this is not the case. The U.S. Supreme Court has acknowledged that the People is mostly a term of art employed in select parts of the Constitution,[41] and has provided differential interpretations of the People in its jurisprudence.[42] In employing the People as an instrumentation, law and the legal process is "made in a field of equations. The issues are the choices as to where the balance is be struck" among competing interests.[43]

[39] Gouverneur Morris described the people (1774) as a "mob [that] began to think and reason. Poor reptiles!" Kramnick, supra note 27 at 23–24.

[40] Erwin Chemerinsky & Michael Stokes Paulsen, Common Interpretation: The Preamble, NAT'L CONST. CTR.: INTERACTIVE CONST., available https://constitutioncenter.org/interactive-constitution/interpretation/preamble-ic/interps/37 (last visited April 18, 2020).

[41] See *U.S. v. Verdugo-Urquidez*, 494 U.S. 259, 265 (1990) ("'[T]he people' seems to have been a term of art employed in select parts of the Constitution. . . . [Its uses] sugges[t] that 'the people' protected by the Fourth Amendment, and by the First and Second Amendments, and to whom rights and powers are reserved in the Ninth and Tenth Amendments, refers to a class of persons who are part of a national community or who have otherwise developed sufficient connection with this country to be considered part of that community.").

[42] See *District of Columbia v. Heller*, 554 U.S. 570, 580 (2008) ("[T]he people' . . . unambiguously refers to all members of the political community, not an unspecified subset.")

[43] Lippmann, supra note 26 at 45.

The People is thus a formal construct from which legitimacy is culled to grant Authority legitimate power. It functions as a macroscopic ordering mechanism, principle, comprised of a distinct constellation of norms and values. The foregoing enables and encourages certain thought and practices, e.g., the profit motive, individual financial hyper-aggrandizement, and an aversion to the redistribution of private wealth and public resources, reflected in law and policy.[44] The People is based on the notion that "representation must not be confused with governing."[45] The People, as a conceptual ordering mechanism, is one that is informed by the operative principle that, "It is possible to govern a state without giving the masses of the people full representation."[46]

The *peoples* provides an alternative normative basis for law and policy that better comports with the of notion of genuine representation in democratic society. Representation, and by extension, fairness, equity, and inclusiveness, entail consideration of diversity of thought and experience based on external societal conditions and problems, such as market-based socioeconomic hierarchy, stratification, and structural poverty, respectively. The *peoples*, therefore, signifies a constellation of norms and values that undergird the socioeconomic actualities of the peoples, wherein the population itself is examined and accounted for in the formulation of policy goals via law and the legal process. The *peoples* is less formal than the People and makes legible and intelligible the complex socioeconomic actualities that directly inform and impact the capacity for those that are emplaced in the lower and lowest socioeconomic sectors of society to exercise fundamental rights. Policy is thus more representative, more inclusive, fair, equitable, and democratic. The is the case because the *peoples* more effectively problematizes the fair and equitable administration of justice. More specifically, the *peoples* more accurately frames the issues and challenges of representation in law and the legal process of those within the lower end of the socioeconomic hierarchy regarding

[44] See, e.g., *Citizens United v. Federal Election Commission*, 558 U.S. 310 (2010) (wherein the Court held that the free speech clause of the First Amendment prohibits government from restricting independent expenditures for political communications by corporations). See also Tim Lau, "Citizens United Explained," Brennan Center for Justice, December 12, 2019, available https://www.brennancenter.org/our-work/research-reports/citizens-united-explained.

[45] Lippmann, supra note 26 at 54.

[46] Id. at 60.

the exercise and application of fundamental rights in the criminal justice context.

There "is a difference between a condition and a problem … Conditions become defined as problems when we come to believe that we should do something about them. Problems are not simply the conditions or external events themselves; there's also a perceptual, interpretive element.… They are great political stakes in problem definition … *How do conditions become defined as problems? Values, comparisons, and categories contribute to the translation.*"[47] How one defines and classifies a problem will have a direct effect on perception, thought, and judgment. Ultimately, judgment is based on values and norms embedded in classification, in discourse, and the processes that perpetuate policy.

Critical examination of law and the interpretive enterprise from a *peoples* perspective, reveals that law encompasses much more than "reasoned elaboration,"[48] and the

> passive discovery of a repository of principles and rights that are representative of and rooted in impersonal principles … positioning the study of law as an 'uncovering' of social purpose for various legal concepts, correlated with an idealized 'purity' of the law outside of the politics of legislation and historical context … Law is far from being divorced from the politics that permeate the constructs and principles of social organization; rather, law is fraught with politics, and reflects a fluid and evolving ulterior state of affairs … The same tension between objectivity and subjectivity exists between the ostensible clarity of the interpretation and end result of law.[49]

Notions of what constitutes a fair, impartial, and equitable legal process are profoundly affected by worldview, which is comprised, in part, of sociocultural, political, and economic norms and values.[50] When

[47] John W. Kingdon, Agendas, Alternatives & Public Policies, Updated 2nd ed., forward James A. Thurber (2011) 109–10 (emphasis added).

[48] See, e.g., Roberto Mangabeira Unger, The Critical Legal Studies Movement: Another Time, A Greater Task (1983) 5.

[49] Marvin L. Astrada & Scott B. Astrada, Law, Continuity & Change: Revisiting the Reasonable Person Within the Demographic, Sociocultural & Political Realities of the 21st Century, 14 *Rutgers J. L. & Pub. Pol'y* 201 (2017), available http://www.rutgerspolicyjournal.org/sites/jlpp/files/Astrada.pdf.

[50] Each society has its regime of truth, it's general politics of truth—that is, "the types of discourse that accepts and makes function as true; the mechanisms and instances that

analyzing the interpretive exercise from a process-based and sociologic and economic view, it is the case that, “Human behavior takes place in relation to a pseudo-environment—a representation, which is not quite the same for any two individuals, of what they suppose to be—not what is—the reality of things. This ... cultural environment, which has its being in the minds of [people,] is interposed between [a subject] as a biological organism and the external reality. It is in this realm that ideas are efficacious. They are efficacious because [people] react to their ideas and images, to their pictures and notions of the world, treating these pictures as if they were the reality.”[51]

B. Binaries & Processes: Unearthing the Affects & Effects of Power

MEF and LAPP provide insight into how the Court constructs the People in its constitutional discourse via its opinions, and the consequences that this has for representative democratic politics. Power relies upon discourse, language—a language that has the consequence of de-emphasizing and reconceptualizing the socioeconomic and political actualities of those that are the subject of discourse. In the case of the Court’s power, it is interesting to note its posture toward the Preamble of the Constitution, textually as well as to the “spirit” of the text:

> Although that preamble indicates the general purposes for which the people ordained and established the Constitution, it has never been regarded as the source of any substantive power conferred on the government of the United States, or on any of its departments. Such powers embrace only those expressly granted in the body of the Constitution, and such as may be implied from those so granted. Although, therefore, one of the declared objects of the Constitution was to secure the blessings of liberty to all under the sovereign jurisdiction and authority of the United States, no power can be exerted to that end by the United States, unless, apart from the preamble, it be found in some express delegation of power, or in some power to be properly implied therefrom. 1 Story, Const. §

enable one to distinguish true and false statements; the means by which each is sanctioned; the techniques and procedures accorded value in the acquisition of truth; the status of those who are charged with saying what counts as true.” Michel Foucault, The Essential Foucault: Selections From Essential Works of Foucault, 1954–1984, ed. Paul Rainbow & Nikolas Rose (1994) 316.

[51] Lippmann, supra note 26 at 92.

> 462. We also pass without discussion the suggestion that the above section of the statute is opposed to the spirit of the Constitution. Undoubtedly, as observed by Chief Justice Marshall, speaking for the court in *Sturges* v. *Crowninshield*, 'the spirit of an instrument, especially of a constitution, is to be respected not less than its letter; yet the spirit is to be collected chiefly from its words.'[52]

The Court assumes the role of supreme wordsmith, utilizing the plasticity of text to procure meaning in accord with its assessment of the meaning to be extracted from the letter and spirit of the text. "Where words conflict with each other, where the different clauses of an instrument bear upon each other, and would be inconsistent, unless the natural and common import of words be varied, construction becomes necessary, and a departure from the obvious meaning of words, is justifiable."[53] The Court has placed itself in the position as supreme expositor of what constitutes the letter and spirit of the Law, and what departures are justifiable, via its compounding the peoples with the People.[54] In the process, it has also assumed control of when and how to bestow constitutionality. In *Planned Parenthood v. Casey*,[55] for instance, it can be argued that the "reality"

[52] *Jacobson v. Massachusetts*, 197 U.S. 11, 22 (1905) (citations omitted).

[53] Sturges v. Crowninshield, 17 U.S. 202 (1819).

[54] "Constitutional law, which speaks today to almost everything, has nothing to say on one subject. It has no account of its own interpretive method. The truth is that most of us don't know if the Supreme Court is 'interpreting' the Constitution at all anymore. Or whether it ever did. Or what exactly it would mean for the Court to do so." Rubenfeld, supra note 9 at 1119, 1120.

[55] At issue in *Casey* were "five provisions of the Pennsylvania Abortion Control Act of 1982: § 3205, which requires that a woman seeking an abortion give her informed consent prior to the procedure, and specifies that she be provided with certain information at least 24 h before the abortion is performed; § 3206, which mandates the informed consent of one parent for a minor to obtain an abortion, but provides a judicial bypass procedure; § 3209, which commands that, unless certain exceptions apply, a married woman seeking an abortion must sign a statement indicating that she has notified her husband; § 3203, which defines a "medical emergency" that will excuse compliance with the foregoing requirements; and §§ 3207(b), 3214(a), and 3214(f), which impose certain reporting requirements on facilities providing abortion services. Before any of the provisions took effect, the petitioners, five abortion clinics and a physician representing himself and a class of doctors who provide abortion services, brought this suit seeking a declaratory judgment that each of the provisions was unconstitutional on its face, as well as injunctive relief. The District Court held all the provisions unconstitutional and permanently enjoined their enforcement. The Court of Appeals affirmed in part and reversed in part, striking down

of poor women was reconfigured by the Court's power to extrapolate meaning and purpose from the constitutional text.[56] The perspective of the Court and its prerogatives take precedence and prevail in the space of constitutional discourse. The Court's power, in part, involves its ability to privilege itself in dialogical space vis-à-vis the actors, issues, and concepts that come before it because it operates in a self-contained, self-defined textual and linguistic universe.[57] In determining what constitutes truth, and by implication falsity, the Court is able to curate its interpretations and convert opinions into truisms. "Really 'the proposition is either true or false' only means that it must be possible to decide for or against it. But this does not say what the ground for such a decision is like."[58] As Justice Scalia notes, "what is unremarkable about the joint opinion's fact-intensive analysis [in *Casey*] is that it does not result in any measurable clarification of the 'undue burden' standard. Rather the approach of the joint opinion is, for the most part, simply to highlight certain facts in the record that apparently strike the three Justices as particularly sufficient in establishing (or refuting) the existence of an undue burden."[59]

the husband notification provision but upholding the others. Held: The judgment in No. 91–902 is affirmed; the judgment in No. 91–744 is affirmed in part and reversed in part, and the case is remanded." *Planned Parenthood of S.E. Pennsylvania v. Casey*, 505 U.S. 833 (1992).

[56] *Planned Parenthood of S.E. Pennsylvania v. Casey*, 505 US 833 (1992). One can claim that the Court personnel's utter disconnectedness with the realities of the lower orders is so stark that it simply cannot understand the basic problems and challenges that so-called "ordinary" people face: "the District Court found that for those women who have the fewest financial resources, those who must travel long distances, and those who have difficulty explaining their whereabouts to husbands, employers, or others, the 24-hour waiting period will be 'particularly burdensome.' *These findings are troubling in some respects, but they do not demonstrate that the waiting period constitutes an undue burden* (emphasis added). *Planned Parenthood of Se. Pennsylvania v. Casey*, 505 U.S. 833, 886 (1992).

[57] See, e.g., *Katzenbach v. Morgan*, 384 U.S. 641, 651 n. 10 (1966) (Congress lacks power "to enact statutes so as in effect to dilute equal protection and due process decisions of this Court."); *Webster v. Reproductive Health Servs.*, 492 U.S. 490, 518 (1989) (plurality opinion of Rehnquist, C.J.) ("Stare decisis is a cornerstone of our legal system, but it has less power in constitutional cases, where, save for constitutional amendments, this Court is the only body able to make needed changes.").

[58] Ludwig Wittgenstein, Major Works, ed. G.E.M. Anscombe & G.H. von Wright (2009) 354.

[59] *Planned Parenthood of S.E. Pennsylvania v. Casey*, 505 U.S. 833, 991–92 (1992). "The inherently standard-less nature of this inquiry invites the district judge to give effect

The test maker therefore controls the material being tested, as well as the means of testing. Legal models become the standard by which the reality of the people is converted to the Court's interpretation of the realities of the people via the People. As noted by the Court in its Casey opinion, "the District Court found that for those women who have the fewest financial resources, those who must travel long distances, and those who have difficulty explaining their whereabouts to husbands, employers, or others, the 24–hour waiting period will be 'particularly burdensome.' These findings are troubling in some respects, but they do not demonstrate that the waiting period constitutes an undue burden."[60] The real, the actual state of affairs that inform the empirical reality of the people is thus appropriated, adjudged, and manufactured on the basis of the Court's notion of the People. The "voice" of the people, from a democratic society and representative politics perspective, in conformity with the notion that the "voice of state authority were none other than the voice of the people itself,"[61] is appropriated, in part, by the Court via models and testing. Testing

> depends on the shifting of the activities underlying [it]. Fundamentally there is no reason why a thing should be done one way rather than another, except as we find it in the very activities themselves. The person accustomed to our marriage laws [, e.g.,] looks upon them as 'natural,' and thinks other nation's queer and needing explanation. Our own he accepts as though they did not need explanation at all. And yet no outside [a] test will give one the advantage over the other. The test must be in the activity itself."[62]

In all configurations of power and order, however, there is no objective "meta-language… that [can] ground political and ethical decisions

to his personal preferences about abortion. By finding and relying upon the right facts, he can invalidate, it would seem, almost any abortion restriction that strikes him as 'undue'—subject, of course, to the possibility of being reversed by a court of appeals or Supreme Court that is as unconstrained in reviewing his decision as he was in making it." Id.

[60] *Planned Parenthood of S.E. Pennsylvania v. Casey*, 505 U.S. 833, 886 (1992).

[61] Rubenfeld, supra note 9 at 1119, 1120.

[62] Arthur F. Bentley, The Process of Government 293 (1908). See also Jacques Derrida, "Structure, Sign and Play in the Discourse of the Human Sciences," in Writing and Difference, trans. Alan Bass (1978) 278–294).

that will be taken as the basis of its statements. There is no metalanguage; there are only genres of language, genres of discourse."[63] All testing, and the means by which things are confirmed or rejected, already occurs within the parameters of the test criteria as posited by the test maker.[64] As Lyotard observes, "no maker of statements, no utterer, is ever autonomous. On the contrary an utterer is always someone who is first of all an addressee ... he is someone who, before he is the utterer of a prescription, has been the recipient of a prescription, and that he is merely a relay; he has also been the object of a prescription."[65] Herein lies a powerful basis for the legitimacy and authority of the Court to declare the fundamental law.

The People can thus be viewed as an elitist construct, a process dominated by discrete and insular elites, grounded in the augmentation, preservation, and perpetuation of the overarching constitutional system as the Court defines its parameters. The nationalist-based People that emerges from *McCulloch v. Maryland* has persisted in the Court's jurisprudence.[66] The nationalist notion of the People is one that has provided a basis for an imagined community. "What kinds of stories inspire people to embrace membership in a particular political community? ... Ethically constitutive stories claim that membership in a particular people is somehow inherent in who the members truly are, in ways that are ethically valuable. Most racial, religious, ethnic, cultural, linguistic, historical, and gendered senses of community membership, among others,

[63] Jean Francois Lyotard and Jean-Loup Thebaud, Just Gaming, trans. Wlad Godzich (1999) 28. As Wittgenstein notes, "If a thought were correct a priori, it would be a thought whose possibility ensured its truth. A priori knowledge that a thought was true would be possible only if its truth were recognizable from the thought itself (without anything to compare it with)." Ludwig Wittgenstein, Tractatus Logico-Philosophicus, trans. D.F. Pears & B.F. McGuiness (1975) 13.

[64] Ludwig Wittgenstein, On Certainty, ed. G.E.M. Anscombe & G.H. Von Wright, trans. Denis Paul & G.E.M. Anscombe (1969) 16.

[65] Lyotard, "Gaming," supra note 63 at 31. See, e.g., Veronica Rocha and Brandon Tensley, CNN's LGBTQ Town Hall, CNN, October 11, 2019, available https://www.cnn.com/politics/live-news/lgbtq-town-hall-2019/index.html.

[66] See, e.g., Richard E. Ellis, Aggressive Nationalism: McCulloch v. Maryland and the Foundation of Federal Authority in the Young Republic (2007).

are ethically constitutive accounts."[67] John Jay provides an ethically constituted imagined nationalist-based People for public consumption:

> It is not a new observation that the people of any country (if, like the Americans, intelligent and well-informed) seldom adopt and steadily persevere for many years in an erroneous opinion respecting their interests. That consideration naturally tends to create great respect for the high opinion which the people of America have so long and uniformly entertained of the importance of their continuing firmly united under one federal government, vested with sufficient powers for all general and national purposes. The more attentively I consider and investigate the reasons which appear to have given birth to this opinion, the more I become convinced that they are cogent and conclusive. Among the many objects to which a wise and free people find it necessary to direct their attention, that of providing for their SAFETY seems to be the first. The SAFETY of the people doubtless has relation to a great variety of circumstances and considerations, and consequently affords great latitude to those who wish to define it precisely and comprehensively.[68]

The Court engages in the same act of imagination, also putting forth ethically constitutive interpretations of the people in order to create a nexus betwixt it and the populace via positing of the People.[69]

C. Contextualizing Power: Court Opinions & People-Based Discourse

Court opinions, in essence, are reflective of an imagined universal state of affairs with objective limited and sovereign underpinnings. "It is imagined because the members of [the political community the Court "serves"] will never know most of their fellow-members, meet them, or even hear them, yet in the minds of each lives the image of their

[67] Rogers M. Smith, "Identities, Interests, and the Future of Political Science, *Perspectives on Politics*, vol. 2, no. 2 (June 2004) 309.

[68] Federalist no. 3 (John Jay), available https://avalon.law.yale.edu/18th_century/fed03.asp

[69] See the discussion of the Court's interpretation of general welfare and its effect on government and governance in John C. Eastman, Restoring the General to the General Welfare Clause, 4 *Chap. L. Rev.* 63 (2001).

communion."[70] The Court speaks for all in its expositions of the Constitution's meaning, purpose, and application. To address the question of the People, one must critically examine the context in which the question is asked, and how context frames and constrains the relationship between the People and government. MEF and LAPP provide insight into the structural context in which the People are defined and utilized in constitutional discourse. The People is a multidimensional concept. It is the repository of a formal identity. It is part of the basis of the Constitution—it undergirds ordering principles and concepts, such as ROL, authority, and legitimacy, that operationalize constitutional government and governance. Promoting and protecting public confidence in government, in the Court, is central to continued faith in ROL and the integrity of the constitutional order as promulgated by the Court.[71] "Constitutions are but a special form of law. They are specially guarded habitual activities of the society, enforcing themselves on all would-be variants ... In the US, constitutions have a special technique, different from statute law, but in subject-matter they overlap at many points."[72] The State, of which the Court is a part, acts in the name of the People it serves. In so doing, an imbrication of the State, its components, the elite that manages it, and the peoples occurs.[73] In the case of the Judicial branch, viz., the Supreme Court, there are three basic ways that constitutional law seeks to give voice to, and make visible, the people, i.e., "through an

[70] Benedict Anderson, Imagined Communities (1991) 6.

[71] See, e.g., Richard H. Fallon, Jr., The Supreme Court's Legitimacy Dilemma: Law & Legitimacy in the Supreme Court; Bob Woodward and Scott Armstrong, The Brethren (1979) 516–18.

[72] Bentley, supra note 62 at 295.

[73] See Smith, supra note 67 at 304. Note how elites wield significant power in shaping the public mind, and contouring the public's and the People's identity, thought, and conduct: "Samuel Chase preached an even stronger line in charging a Pennsylvania Grand Jury. 'The Judicial Power,' he said, 'are the only proper and competent authority to decide whether any Law made by Congress; or any of the State Legislatures is contrary to or in Violation of the federal Constitution.' Chase, too, was as good as his word when presiding at trial—lecturing John Fries that questions of constitutionality were the sole province of the judiciary as he sentenced him to death for leading a mob protest against federal taxes, and refusing to permit Thomas Callendar's defense attorney to argue to the jury the unconstitutionality of the Sedition Act." Larry D. Kramer, Marbury and the Retreat from Judicial Supremacy, 605 Constitutional Commentary 221 (2003), available https://scholarship.law.umn.edu/concomm/605.

originalist, process-based, or values-based approach."[74] Each approach, whether focusing on the intent of the framers, safeguarding democratic processes, or having judges articulates "evolving constitutional ideals" (originalist, process-based, and fundamental-values approaches, respectively),[75] relies upon the conversion of the people into the People by the Court. This is the case because the People conforms to the Court's rules of formation and reality principles when positing constitutional meaning and truth.

When taken as a self-evident or common-sense concept or construct, the People functions as a relatively stable notion that expresses itself through a democratic "General Will."[76] In the realm of representation and public policy, however, the People is a very problematic concept. Representation is quite complex, especially in a nation of 330 million people.[77] It can be viewed in different ways, viz., in a universalist or pluralistic community-based framework, which results in very distinctive paradigms for characterizing representation. Liberalism, which underpins American norms pertaining to politics and economy, is individualistic, celebrating difference.

> [B]ecause individual ends are not homogeneous, they are incompatible with the existence of an overarching common end. But the universalist assumption at the base of liberal thought is that, because humans are identical in their status as moral beings, moral obligation cannot be contingent on individual attributes, merits, or circumstances. The liberal conception

[74] Rubenfeld, supra note 9 at 1119, 1121.

[75] Id.

[76] See Philip J. Kain, Rousseau, the General Will, and Individual Liberty, *History of Philosophy Quarterly*, vol. 7, no. 3 (July 1990) 315–34.

[77] "While one must agree with Justice Breyer's incredibly abstract starting point that our Constitution sought to create a 'basically democratic' form of government, that is a long and impassable distance away from the conclusion that the Judiciary may assess whether a group (somehow defined) has achieved a level of political power (somehow defined) commensurate with that to which they would be entitled absent *unjustified* political machinations (whatever that means)." *Vieth v. Jubelirer*, 541 U.S. 267, 299 (2004).

> of the moral equality of persons requires that law have universal application: it must treat all persons identically and disinterestedly, and its grant of rights and liberties must extend to all persons.[78]

Pluralism, on the other hand, celebrates and embraces group difference. Each poses challenges to the establishment, exposition, and expression of a singular nationalist-based People.[79]

Representation in U.S. national society is profoundly challenging given the diversity and difference that permeates the national landscape, e.g., regionally, politically, ideologically, socioeconomically, and socioculturally. The tension between mass and elite, the sociocultural and economic disconnect betwixt the two, and the very different experiential actualities that underpin each state of affairs, render actual representation of a substantial portion of the polity profoundly challenging. Those that are emplaced on the mid to lower level sectors of the socioeconomic and political system "have to spend a great deal of imaginative energy trying to understand the social dynamics that surround them—including having to imagine the perspectives of those on top—while the latter can wander about largely oblivious to much of what is going on around them."[80] Difference permeates norms, values, morals, and other ideational ordering mechanisms that enable a group or groups of people to effectively cohere around a stable and universalizable set of ordering concepts and principles, such as ROL. As J.S. Mill observes, "The 'people' who exercise

[78] Note, The Myth of Context in Politics and Law, 110 *Harv. L. Rev.* 1292, 1294 (1997). See also Thomas Morawetzt, Understanding Disagreement—The Root Issue of Jurisprudence: Applying Wittgenstein To Positivism, Critical Theory & Judging, 141 *U. Pa. L. Rev.* 375, n. 5 (1992–1993). "Many writers go further and characterize liberal assumptions about value consensus as devious and repressive. The dominant groups in society, on this view, universalize their interests and experience and repress the self-expression of groups (e.g. women and minorities) without power. According to Robert Gordon, one can represent law as a legitimating ideology in the view that '[t]he ruling class induces consent and demobilizes opposition by masking its role in widely shared utopian norms and fair procedures, which it then distorts to its own purposes' ... Gordon himself seems to proffer an account wherein these preferences are concealed even from the actors themselves because '[t]he discourse of law-its categories, arguments, reasoning modes, rhetorical tropes, and procedural rituals-fits into a complex of discursive practices that together structure how people perceive.'" Id.

[79] See Isaiah Berlin, Ethical Thought and Value Pluralism, Stanford Encyclopedia of Philosophy, available https://plato.stanford.edu/archives/win2016/entries/berlin/#5.4.

[80] David Graeber, The Utopia of Rules (2015) 49, available https://libcom.org/files/David_Graeber-The_Utopia_of_Rules_On_Technology_St.pdf.

the power are not always the same people with those over whom it is exercised."[81]

In the interpretive enterprise of the fundamental law, it is the case that the Justices are very far removed from the lives of the mass of the American people. Socioeconomically, culturally, and politically, the Justices (and federal judges) have very little in common with the mass they ostensibly represent, serve, and speak for.

> The educated elite of America have a different set of opinions and values than the rest of the country – not always, but as a rule. The divide between the educated elite and the rest of the nation, on a wide range of legally relevant issues, is bigger than that between men and women, and possibly bigger than divides based on race or religion. By granting the Judiciary the kind of authority it has to invalidate legislation passed by elected bodies, is to give the educated elite a veto over actions that have been approved politically by the representatives of the American citizenry. The Judiciary, some scholars note, is not unlike the House of Lords.[82]

Despite the chasm betwixt the people and Court, the Court is nonetheless able to declare that it "is confronted with the task of reconciling conflicting rights of the diverse communities within our society and of

[81] J.S. Mill, On Liberty, available http://www.gutenberg.org/ebooks/34901.

[82] Michael W. McConnell, What Are the Judiciary's Politics? 45 *Pepp. L. Rev.* 455, 458–59 (2018). When the Founders articulated the superstructure for an American Political and National community and refer to the People, "they think of it always as legitimately represented by its 'natural' leaders," whom Medieval philosophers and political theorists designated the "*selecti*, *ephori* … The idea that each separate individual should have an equal share in the exercise of sovereignty" is a relatively recent invention. Mosca, supra note 32 at 380–81. If this is the case, and it seems to be, then does the People need to be revisited, revaluated, and reconfigured to meet the actualities that constitute the present, and in which the notion of representative politics is subject to interpolation due to the massive changes that characterize the present polity, and the tension that has emerged from a populist/elitist context? Have the elite of government assumed the role of the natural leader in the conduct of politics and policy? "In spite of the gradual adoption of universal suffrage, actual power has remained partly in the hands of the wealthiest classes, and in larger part still, especially in so-called democratic countries, in the hands of the [upper] middle classes. Those classes have always had the upper hand in the controlling cliques of political parties and in electioneering committees, and they have supplied in large part, the reporting and editorial staffs of the daily press [and] the personnel of the bureaucracies." Id. at 389.

individuals."[83] This logically follows when employing a singular, self-referential, (reverential?), and self-contained discourse, that converts the people into the People.

MEF and LAPP highlight the role of socioeconomic, cultural, political, and ideological factors in the manufacture of the People. The United States "exists as a sovereign nation with its officially stated Constitution, its economic and foreign policies, its demarcated, patrolled boundaries. 'America,' however, exists as image or idea, as dream or nightmare, as romance or plague, constructed by discrete individual fantasies, and shaded by collective paranoias and mythologies."[84] The concept of a General Will (nor its liberal and plural underpinnings) cannot be comprehensibly summarized in the limited space of this work, but for the purpose of our discussion, it is problematic in the realms of representation and public policy because, as Bruno Bosteeles observes, there is no People before the act by which a people becomes the People in the first place. "[T]he people are never one or homogenous but many and internally divided. In sum, far from constituting a stable identity derived from a preordained essence that would have been racially, ethnically, linguistically, culturally, or ontologically definable," the People serves as a place-name for a political and legal process "that produces its own subject, while reminding us that without subjectivation there can be no politics."[85]

The question then becomes essentially a political, cultural, and ideological one, and thus, subject to critical analysis on how a polity, and the People (or a subsection of it), is conceptualized in law and politics. The question of who exactly are the People is one of the power and

[83] *Jacobellis v. Ohio*, 378 U.S. 184, 200–1 (1964).

[84] Bharati Mukherjee, "Beyond Multiculturalism," in Multi-America: Essays on Cultural Wars & Cultural Peace, ed. Ishmael Reed (1998) 454.

[85] Bruno Bosteels, Introduction in "What Is a People?" by Alain Badiou, et al. (2016) 20. See also *Tennessee Power Co. v. T.V.A.*, 306 U.S. 118, 137, 143–44 (1939) (wherein the Court found that when invoking the "doctrine that one threatened with direct and special injury by the act of an agent of the government which, but for statutory authority for its performance, would be a violation of his legal rights, may challenge the validity of the statute in a suit against the agent ... is without application unless the right invaded is a legal right—one of property, one arising out of contract, one protected against tortious invasion, or one founded on a statute which confers a privilege."); *Griswold v. Connecticut*, 381 U.S. 479, 484 (1965) (wherein the Court found that "specific guarantees in the Bill of Rights have penumbras, formed by emanations from those guarantees that help give them life and substance.")

privilege to identify what exactly constitutes the criteria of Peoplehood. As noted earlier, in Federalist no. 10, James Madison explicitly articulates the elitist foundation for government and governance to protect the opulent minority from "the superior force of an interested and overbearing majority"[86] (that is, the peoples). The minute subsection of the opulent that possesses the ability to define—and associate itself as a protector of—the People is one correlated with elite sociocultural, political, and economic status. For instance, legal citizenship, which only the Sovereign can provide, provides "a sense of belonging to a territorialized political community most often represented by the nation-state. Citizenship, in this respect, offers a bounded [space] that reflects the historical articulation of national communities ... Citizenship serves ...

[86]Federalist no. 10 (James Madison), available https://avalon.law.yale.edu/18th_century/fed10.asp. Madison goes on to declare and justify 1., how the factious nature of the minority and majority interests informs the blueprint for American government and governance and 2., the structural socioeconomic-based stratification of the polity that the fundamental preserves via the fundamental law: "By a faction, I understand a number of citizens, whether amounting to a majority or a minority of the whole, who are united and actuated by some common impulse of passion, or of interest, adversed to the rights of other citizens, or to the permanent and aggregate interests of the community ... The diversity in the faculties of men, from which the rights of property originate, is not less an insuperable obstacle to a uniformity of interests. The protection of these faculties is the first object of government. From the protection of different and unequal faculties of acquiring property, the possession of different degrees and kinds of property immediately results; and from the influence of these on the sentiments and views of the respective proprietors, ensues a division of the society into different interests and parties ... he most common and durable source of factions has been the various and unequal distribution of property. Those who hold and those who are without property have ever formed distinct interests in society. Those who are creditors, and those who are debtors, fall under a like discrimination. A landed interest, a manufacturing interest, a mercantile interest, a moneyed interest, with many lesser interests, grow up of necessity in civilized nations, and divide them into different classes, actuated by different sentiments and views. The regulation of these various and interfering interests forms the principal task of modern legislation, and involves the spirit of party and faction in the necessary and ordinary operations of the government ... the majority ... must be rendered, by their number and local situation, unable to concert and carry into effect schemes of oppression. If the impulse and the opportunity be suffered to coincide, we well know that neither moral nor religious motives can be relied on as an adequate control. They are not found to be such on the injustice and violence of individuals, and lose their efficacy in proportion to the number combined together, that is, in proportion as their efficacy becomes needful. " Id.

as a mode of inclusion and incorporation in society and as a legal and cultural framework."[87]

Policy spaces reflect the politics that attaches to elite government and nongovernmental actors defining the American People. In the case of immigration, for instance, the notion of an American People is a product of, in part, the Executive's substantial control over the legal regime governing which type of people qualify to enter and remain in the United States, with Congressional delegation of power and Court deference to said delegation.[88] Employing a MEF and LAPP lens highlights the racial, ethnic, economic class, religious, and ideological classifications that undergird the People. Each illuminates the fact that the People is thus not necessarily a representative concept in a democratic sense of the term. In the case of the Supreme Court, the foregoing is expressed in light of the elitist and nondemocratic nature of the Court's power to distill and proclaim the fundamental law.

[87] Caroline R. Nagel and Lynn A. Staeheli, Citizenship, Identity, and Transnational Migration: Arab Immigrants to the US, *Space and Polity*, vol. 8, no. 1 2004) 3–24, 5.

[88] See *US ex rel. Knauff v. Shaughnessy*, 338 U.S. 537, 542 (1950) (wherein the Court found that, "exclusion of aliens is a fundamental act of sovereignty. The right to do so stems not alone from legislative power but is inherent in the executive power to control the foreign affairs of the nation."). The courts, before and after Shaughnessy, have been deferential to the Executive in the realms of national security and immigration based, in part, on Congressional delegation of its immigration power over to the Executive. In *Kleindienst v. Mandel*, 408 U.S. 753, 770 (1972) the Court stated that, within the immigration context, the courts should not "look behind the exercise of [Executive] discretion" when exercised "on the basis of a facially legitimate and bona fide reason." See also *Galvan v. Press*, 347 U.S. 522, 531 (1954); see also U.S. Const. art. I, § 8, cl. 4 ("The Congress shall have Power ... [t]o establish an uniform Rule of Naturalization..."); *Fiallo v. Bell*, 430 U.S. 787, 792, 796 (1977) ("[O]ver no conceivable subject is the legislative power of Congress more complete than it is over the admission of aliens ... The conditions of entry for every alien, the particular classes of aliens that shall be denied entry altogether, the basis for determining such classification ... have been recognized as matters solely for the responsibility of the Congress. . .") (internal quotation marks omitted); Furthermore, in the Immigration and Nationalization Act of 1952, Congress delegated power to the President through Sect. 212(f), which provides, in part that, "Whenever the President finds that the entry of any aliens or of any class of aliens into the United States would be detrimental to the interests of the United States, he may by proclamation, and for such period as he shall deem necessary, suspend the entry of all aliens or any class of aliens as immigrants or nonimmigrants, or impose on the entry of aliens any restrictions he may deem to be appropriate." 8 U.S.C. § 1182(f).

Court discourse reifies its interpretation of the People in its jurisprudence, espousing the authenticity of the People via a normative association of its interpretation with an objective referent.[89] That is, the Court equivocates its use of the People (conceptual construct) with the actual people (empirical state of affairs) of the U.S. Alain Badiou defines the notion of a People (in his example, the French People) "in reality mean[ing] nothing more than 'the inert mass of those upon whom the state has conferred the right to call themselves French.'"[90] The process of legitimizing the normative association for a subset of the polity to be or have the power to define the People is, in part, effectuated by the process of identification with a reflection of what type of person or group is the basis of the interests that the elite at the upper echelon of power hold. The Court assumes this role for the judicial branch. This is why the Court was able to boldly state, in the case of abortion, that,

> Where, in the performance of its judicial duties, the Court decides a case in such a way as to resolve the sort of intensely divisive controversy reflected in Roe and those rare, comparable cases, its decision has a dimension that the resolution of the normal case does not carry. It is the dimension present *whenever the Court's interpretation of the Constitution calls the contending sides of a national controversy to end their national division by accepting a common mandate rooted in the Constitution.*[91]

The will of the People is an essential aspect of the legitimate exercise of power to declare a singular interpretation of the fundamental law. The "people it claims as its authority ... becomes a passive mass that the [Court] configures, universally."[92] In demanding that the American People "end their national division by accepting a common mandate rooted in the Constitution," the Court engages in a two-level process, whereby the polity is 1., fractured into distinct communities and identities, and 2., while certain minute subsets of the whole have the privilege

[89] See John Agnew, Mapping Political Power Beyond State Boundaries: Territory, Identity and Movement in World Politics, *Millennium: Journal of International Studies*, vol. 28, no. 3 (1999) 499–521 .

[90] Bosteels, supra note 85 at 23–24.

[91] *Planned Parenthood of S.E. Pennsylvania v. Casey*, 505 U.S. 833, 866–67 (1992) (emphasis added).

[92] Bosteels, supra note 85 at 25–26.

of identifying the character and content of the People rooted in the fundamental law.

The People thus function as the bedrock of legitimate justification for the State to act on behalf of People. The Court, it must be noted, is government, and government is the State. This fact seems to be lost at times in mainstream political discourse, which treats the Court as if it actually stands outside of the political, ideological, and sociocultural complexities that permeate the other branches of government. The enduring (myth of) presence of objectivity in the Law is captured in the confirmation hearing remarks of U.S. Supreme Court Chief Justice Roberts: "Judges and Justices are servants of the law, not the other way around. Judges are like umpires. Umpires don't make the rules, they apply them. The role of an umpire and a judge is critical. They make sure everybody plays by the rules, but it is a limited role."[93] The legitimized expression of the General Will through the electoral system, on all levels of government minus the Court, still does not reconcile the exclusionary nature of the People, because "it is never really the case that all of the possible people who are represented by 'the people' show up to claim they are the people! So 'we, the people' always has its constitutive outside, as we know. It is this surely not the fact that the 'we' fairly and fully represents all the people; it cannot, even though it can strive for more inclusive aims."[94] Representation, in any substantive degree, is ablated in the exercise of Court power. The Court, unaccountably, is able to pronounce judgment on every facet of a subject's legal actuality as

[93] Confirmation Hearing on the Nomination of John G. Roberts, Jr. to be Chief Justice of the United States, September 12–15, 2005. Transcript available at https://www.govinfo.gov/content/pkg/gpo-chrg-roberts/pdf/gpo-chrg-roberts.pdf. See also Adam Liptak, "Chief Justice Defends Judicial Independence After Trump Attacks 'Obama Judge,'" New York Times, Nov. 21, 2018, available https://www.nytimes.com/2018/11/21/us/politics/trump-chief-justice-roberts-rebuke.html. "Chief Justice John G. Roberts Jr. defended the independence and integrity of the federal judiciary on Wednesday, rebuking President Trump for calling a judge who had ruled against his administration's asylum policy 'an Obama judge.' The chief justice said that was a profound misunderstanding of the judicial role. 'We do not have Obama judges or Trump judges, Bush judges or Clinton judges,' he said in a statement. 'What we have is an extraordinary group of dedicated judges doing their level best to do equal right to those appearing before them. That independent judiciary is something we should all be thankful for.'" Id.

[94] Bosteels, supra note 85 at 53.

the final word on the fundamental law, where one views the outcomes as "good" or "bad."[95]

The People, then, in a democratic society, is not a homogenizing concept by which the distilling of a General Will takes place, but rather "a set of debates about who the people are and what they want."[96] This dimension is absent in Court discourse regarding the larger democratic process and representative political system.[97] When viewing the People through the lenses of MEF and LAPP, wherein the elite hold plenary or a preponderance of power, influence, and control over public policy, the process of democratic representation is stretched thin considering the fact that, the "people who are the 'we' do something other than represent themselves as the people, and this act of self-making or self-constitution is not the same as any form of representation [...] This act of self-designating and self-constituting forms as assembly that articulates itself as the 'people.' Popular sovereignty is thus a form of self-making that is separate from the very representative regime it legitimates."[98] In the administration of justice, then, the Court cannot "concern itself with correcting every injustice ... [It must always] consider the big picture."[99]

[95] See, e.g., *Dred Scott v. Sandford*, 60 U.S. 393 (1857) and Plessy v. Ferguson, 163 U.S. 537 (1896), contrasted with *Brown v. Board of Education of Topeka*, 347 U.S. 483 (1954), *Miranda v. Arizona*, 384 U.S. 436 (1966) and *Gideon v. Wainwright*, 372 U.S. 335 (1963).

[96] Bosteels, supra note 85 at 53. See James L. Gibson and Michael J. Nelson, Is the U.S. Supreme Court's Legitimacy Grounded in Performance Satisfaction and Ideology?*American Journal of Political Science*, vol. 59, no. 1 (January 2015) 162–174.

[97] See Maxwell L. Stearns, Direct (Anti-)democracy, 80 *Geo. Wash. L. Rev.* 311, 326 (2012) (analyzing the benefits and pitfalls of direct democracy). See also *City of Eastlake v. Forest City Enterprises, Inc.*, 426 U.S. 668, 668 (1976) (wherein the Court found that a referendum, which is a means for direct political participation by the people, allowing them what amounts to a veto power over legislative enactments, cannot be characterized as a delegation of power. In establishing legislative bodies, the people can reserve to themselves power to deal directly with matters that might otherwise be assigned to the legislature.). Id.

[98] Bosteels, supra note 85 at 53. See Morgan Marietta, A Citizen's Guide to the Constitution and the Supreme Court: Constitutional Conflict in American Politics (2014).

[99] Woodward, supra note 71 at 272. The quote refers to the case of *Moore v. Illinois*, 408 U.S. 786 (1972) (finding that defendant's right to due process was not violated by state's failure to produce evidence that one witness had misidentified defendant and other evidence contradicting such identification, where such evidence did not impeach identification of defendant as murder victim's assailant, so that the misidentification was not material to issue of guilt. Also, the Court found that prosecution for murder allegedly

Court power has a tendency, it seems, to cast the polity as a passive, singular-willed body of subjects with homogenous interests. This is the opposite of a "we the people" that "does not describe the plurality but seeks to bring about the social plurality that speaks it."[100] The Court's discourse is the bedrock of its power; perceptions of its legitimacy hinge on the integrity of the textual interpretations of fundamental law proffered for public consumption. "[L]anguage implies a specific metaphysics of life. The interpretation defines our relations to ... other human beings and to the self."[101] To effectively perpetuate review and supremacy, Court power selectively formalizes the expression of the People's will. This is an inherently political and ideological process, with consequences for representative politics. "Many of the Court decisions, perhaps all of them, [have] political repercussions of one kind or another."[102] Thus, the question of who are the People "is never the affirmation of a pre-given identity, never a self-fulfilling prophecy—it is always the production of an image of identity and the transformation of the subject assuming the image."[103] Thus, the Court transforms the American population comprised of the people into the People when it expresses the latter's will.

The question of who are the People remains a political and ideological one. Take, for example, the case of *Warth v. Seldin*, 422 U.S. 490 (1975) (wherein plaintiff's claimed that the town's zoning ordinance effectively excluded persons of low and moderate income from living in the town, in contravention of petitioners' constitutional rights and in violation of civil rights statutes), in which the Court reiterated and upheld

> limits on the class of persons who may invoke the courts' decisional and remedial powers ... when the asserted harm is a 'generalized grievance' shared in substantially equal measure by all or a large class of citizens,

committed with 12-gauge shotgun, admission into evidence of 16-gauge shotgun which was in constructive possession of defendant and another when they were arrested was not so irrelevant or inflammatory as to deprive defendant of due process).

[100] Bosteels, supra note 85 at 53. See Alexander M. Bickel, The Least Dangerous Branch: The Supreme Court at the Bar of Politics (1962) 18.

[101] Jeff Huysmans, Security! What Do You Mean? From Concept to Thick Signifier, *European Journal of International Relations*, vol. 4, no. 2 (January 1998): 226–55, 231.

[102] Woodward, supra note 71 at 418.

[103] Homi K. Bhabha, The Location of Culture (1994) 64.

> that harm alone normally does not warrant exercise of jurisdiction[, and] even when the plaintiff has alleged injury sufficient to meet the 'case or controversy' requirement, this Court has held that the plaintiff generally must assert his own legal rights and interests, and cannot rest his claim to relief on the legal rights or interests of third parties. Without such limitations—closely related to Art. III concerns but essentially matters of judicial self-governance—the courts would be called upon to decide abstract questions of wide public significance even though other governmental institutions may be more competent to address the questions and even though judicial intervention may be unnecessary to protect individual rights.[104]

Justice Stewart expounded upon *Warth*'s reasoning and holding, concluding that, "the case called for a value judgement, not a legal one. The challengers were asking the courts ultimately to rule on economic differences that kept low income minorities from living near affluent whites. What they are really asking us to do is overrule the capitalist system."[105]

Under *Warth*'s reasoning, the People, its will, and fundamental rights take on a very specific, restricted, and select interpretation. Sociocultural and economic stratification is a norm, a natural trait of the People. In the case of *Warth*, Justice Powell also noted that, "poor minorities were the victims, not of zoning law, but of the economics of the housing market, something the courts could do nothing about."[106] Whether or not one agrees with the Court's ruling, it is the power to mold the people, declare its limits, boundaries, and contours that should be the focus of critical inquiry.[107] The Court, as a political actor, possesses an

[104] *Warth v. Seldin*, 422 U.S. 490, 499–500 (1975).

[105] Woodward, supra note 71 at 444.

[106] Id. Justice Brenan, on the other hand, noted that, for "the poor to sue, they had to be rich ... it was the ordinance being challenged—not neutral economic factors—that insured that the housing market would never change." Id. at 445.

[107] See also *United States v. Kras*, 409 U.S. 434, 459–60 (1973) (Marshall, J., dissenting): "I cannot agree with the majority that it is so easy for the desperately poor to save $1.92 each week over the course of six months ... I see no reason to require that families in such straits sacrifice over 5% of their annual income as a prerequisite to getting a discharge in bankruptcy. It may be easy for some people to think that weekly savings of less than $2 are no burden. But no one who has had close contact with poor people can fail to understand how close to the margin of survival many of them are. A sudden illness, for example, may destroy whatever savings they may have accumulated, and by

ideological and normative locus from which interpretation flows. MEF and LAPP thus highlight the role of ideology (as it manifests in the manufacture of public policy) in the sociocultural process that informs and contextualizes the fundamental law. The Court's view of political economy in *Warth* is exemplary of this. "Ideology is the foundation of the thought of a class society within the conflictual course of history. Ideological entities have never been mere fictions[;] rather, they are a distorted consciousness of reality, and, as such, real factors retroactively producing real distorting effects."[108]

eliminating a sense of security may destroy the incentive to save in the future. A pack or two of cigarettes may be, for them, not a routine purchase but a luxury indulged in only rarely. The desperately poor almost never go to see a movie, which the majority seems to believe is an almost weekly activity. They have more important things to do with what little money they have—like attempting to provide some comforts for a gravely ill child, as Kras must do. It is perfectly proper for judges to disagree about what the Constitution requires. But it is disgraceful for an interpretation of the Constitution to be premised upon unfounded assumptions about how people live." Id.

[108] Guy Debord, Society of the Spectacle (1995) 61.

CHAPTER 4

Step 4: The People, Process, Law and Court Power

Abstract MEF and LAPP provide a means of disaggregating the anonymity and coherency of Court-produced truths and the methods by which knowledge is converted into a truth regime. Court opinions, as expositions of knowledge and truth, establish a corpus of truth, a regime of truth based on knowledge that the Court applies and obtains through the interpretive process. Court opinions, as epistemic constructs, constitute a textual and ideational structure upon which meaning is produced and constitutionalized. By focusing on the sociocultural, economic, political, and ideological factors that inform the process of Court-produced knowledge and truth—and the methodology by which each is effectuated—the chasm betwixt the Court and the realities that contextualize the actual people the Court "serves" is brought to the fore. Uniformity, unity, and conceptual mechanisms anchored in self-contained textual universe of Court discourse, provide the foundation for an objectively configured and constructed discourse.

Keywords Ideology · Rules of formation · Truth regime · Knowledge · Fundamental law

M. L. Astrada, *Law, Society & Politics*,
https://doi.org/10.1007/978-3-030-66714-6_4

The People is a cornerstone of the Court's power. It is important to note how the Court produces a discourse that is "accepted on [its] own merits and positioned within an anonymous and coherent conceptual system of established truths and methods of verification."[1] The Court's discourse is characterized and presented as a "univocal, deliberate declaration of the voice of the people."[2] The Court has declared that, "'the powers delegated to the federal government are, in all cases, to receive the most strict construction that the instrument will bear, where the rights of a State, or of the people, either collectively or individually, may be drawn in question.' This rule of construction must be correct; for *the constitution gives nothing to the States or to the people*. Their rights existed before it was formed, and are derived from the nature of sovereignty and the principles of freedom."[3] Yet, notions of rights, freedoms, obligations, protections, limits, and responsibilities of subjects rely exclusively upon the Court's interpretation of the Constitution. "Strict construction" has not been the norm, in that the Court has manufactured various rights that do not find expression under a strict construction, such as the right to an abortion,[4] self-defense,[5] marriage,[6] that corporations are entitled to constitutional protections,[7] and the liberty to contract.[8] The manner in which the Court

[1] Michel Foucault, "What Is an Author?" 1622–1636, 1628 (trans. Donald F. Bushard & Sherry Simon in The Norton Anthology of Theory & Criticism, eds. Vincent B. Leitch, et al., 2001).

[2] Jed Rubenfeld, Reading the Constitution as Spoken, 104 *Yale L.J.* 1119, 1122 (1995). Counterexamples of this modality of power in a democratic political system include the following: Hans Kelsen: "The will of the community, in a democracy, is always created through a running discussion between majority and minority; Jürgen Habermas: A democratic politics must strive toward implementation of 'a common will, communicatively shaped and discursively clarified in the political public sphere'; Claude Lefort: "Modern democracy invites us to replace the notion … of a legitimate power, by the notion of a regime founded upon *the legitimacy of a debate as to what is legitimate and what is illegitimate* . …."; Stephen Holmes: "Democracy is government by public discussion." Id. at 1124.

[3] *Gibbons v. Ogden*, 22 U.S. 1, 86–87 (1824).

[4] *Roe v. Wade*, 410 U.S. 113 (1973).

[5] *District of Columbia v. Heller*, 554 U.S. 570 (2008).

[6] *Obergefell v. Hodges*, 576 U.S. 644 (2015).

[7] *Santa Clara County v. Southern Pacific Railroad Company*, 118 U.S. 394 (1886).

[8] *Lochner v. New York*, 198 U.S. 45 (1905).

manufactures rights rather than the "correctness" of the aforementioned rights should control critical analysis of Court power.

MEF and LAPP provide an effective means of disaggregating the anonymity and coherency of Court-produced truths and the methods by which knowledge is converted into a singular truth regime that is univocal and held out as declaring the voice and will of the peoples.[9] Strict construction is not the mainstay of the People, since it lends itself to the ebb and flow of classification-based, in part, on the Court's constituent components. In the case of the peoples, "Self-government is nonsense ... unless the 'self' which governs is able and determined to make its will effective."[10] Court opinions, as expositions of knowledge and truth, establish a corpus of truth, a regime of truth based on knowledge that the Court applies and obtains through the interpretive process.[11] This has a direct impact on the qualities that define a self-governing, democratic representative political system, in light of the Court's power to declare what the Constitution means for the entire polity.

Court opinions, as epistemic constructs, constitute a textual and ideational structure upon which singular meaning is produced and constitutionalized.[12] The Court's equivocation of its interpretations of the fundamental law with the Constitution blurs the purlieus between a subjective and an objective state of affairs, ignoring the fact that "there are no eternal facts, just as there are no absolute truths."[13] The Peoples is more of an ahistorical artifact in that that it has been grafted onto the peoples, dispensing with the variegated complexities immanent in the peoples that simply do not lend themselves to a unitary, univocal, homogenous state of affairs encompassed in the signifier of the People.

[9] See Lorna Weir, The Concept of Truth Regime, *Canadian Journal of Sociology*, vol. 33, no. 2 (2008) 367–389; Jean Jacques Rousseau, The Social Contract Or Principles Of Political Right, trans. G. D. H. Cole ([1762,] 1950), available https://socialpolicy.ucc.ie/Rousseau_contrat-social.pdf.

[10] Alexander Meiklejohn, Political Freedom: The Constitutional Powers of the People (1948) 14.

[11] Marvin L. Astrada & Scott B. Astrada, The Integrity of the Binary: Politics, Identity & the Law in the 21st Century, 17 U. MD. L. J. RACE RELIG. GENDER & CLASS 192 (2017), available http://digitalcommons.law.umaryland.edu/rrgc/vol17/iss2/2/.

[12] See, Jessica Knouse, From Identity Politics to Ideology Politics, 2009 *UTAH L. REV.* 749, 750 (2009).

[13] Friedrich Nietzsche, Human All Too Human: A Book for Free Spirits, trans. R.J. Hollingdale, intro. R. Schact (1996) 13.

Jacques Derrida's consideration of Edmund Husserl's redemption of rationalism and reason is applicable here: "objectivist naïveté is no mere accident. It is produced by the very progress of the sciences and by the production of ideal objects, which, as if by themselves, by their iterability and their necessarily technical structure, cover over or consign to forgetting their historical and subjective origin."[14] This forgetting of origins or imagining a population that can be reduced to basic, formal, and universal principles of construction can be observed in the People. Jacques Derrida sums up the process of naturalizing what is not natural with the metaphor of the silkworm wrapping itself in a cocoon:

> I would be tempted to take somewhat seriously this metaphor of the cocoon [...] that objectivizes, indeed naturalizes a non-natural movement: reason spontaneously envelops itself in the web and threads that it itself weaves after having itself secreted them–like a silkworm. The threads of this web come at once to reveal and veil the unveiling of truth. This reason resembles the *physis* of the silkworm, which, from the inside, on its own, produces and objectivizes on the outside the veil of naturalism and objectivism in which it will shut itself for a time. Up until the point when the heroism of reason makes it appear, resuscitates it, and lets it be reborn."[15]

The objectivity of Court opinions is at base comparable to a cocoon of its own making, and the erasure of a subject's history is the erasure of the recognition of the historicity and subjectivity that undergird constitutional interpretation.

The question posed by Patrick Henry regarding the use of the People in the Constitution's Preamble is as relevant today as it was during the founding: "What right had they to say, We, the people? My political curiosity, exclusive of my anxious solicitude for the public welfare, leads me to ask, who authorized them to speak the language of We, the people ..."[16] This sentiment and critique finds continual expression in the modern context—"Different cultures and lifestyles in America use the same words with different shades of meaning[, such as "free enterprise," "the profit system," "individualism," and "competition."] All

[14] Jacques Derrida, *Rogue States*, trans. Pascale-Ann Brault & Michael Naas (2005) 126.

[15] Id. at 130–31.

[16] Patrick Henry, quoted in Herbert J. Storing, What the Anti-Federalists Were For: The Political Thought of the Opponents of the Constitution (1981) 12.

belong to one society yet live in different worlds."[17] By focusing on the sociocultural, economic, political, and ideological factors that inform the process of Court-produced knowledge and truth—and the methodology by which each is effectuated—the chasm betwixt the Court and the realities that contextualize the actual people the Court "serves" is brought to the fore. The self-contained, self-referential, and self-reverential logic of Court interpretations of the fundamental law become legible in constitutional discourse. Uniformity, unity, and conceptual mechanisms anchored in self-contained textual universe of Court discourse, provide the foundation for an objectively configured and constructed discourse. Language, discourse, and thought are modalities for the exercise of power, control—each facilitates a paradigm wherein "there is nothing outside of the"[18] discourse of Court power when it comes to the fundamental law.[19] Review and supremacy, as the basic analytic building blocks of the American Constitution as interpreted by a supreme and incontestable judicial authority, create and disseminate very specific rules of formation for constitutional discourse and actuality. Rules "of formation are conditions of existence (but also of coexistence, maintenance, modification, and disappearance) in a given discursive action."[20]

Arrangements of order prescribe rules of being, modalities of existence, through classification of what rights, limitations, freedoms, obligations, etc., constitute the legal and constitutional actuality for 331 million people. In practice, it seems, the Constitution, as the singular textual source of truth is a "euphemistic fiction that performs the function of diplomatic obfuscation. And it is arguably the capacity of language, and of a common term, to beguile us into thinking that we are committed to a common object—the Constitution—that helps us get along as well

[17] Huey P. Newton, The Huey P. Newton Reader, ed. David Hilliard & Donald Weise (2002) 36, 74.

[18] Jacques Derrida, "Grammatology," trans. Gayatri Spivak in The Norton Anthology of Theory & Criticism, ed. Vincent B. Leitch, et al. (2001) 1822–1830, 1825.

[19] See William H. Rehnquist, Constitutional Law and Public Opinion, 20 *SUFFOLK U. L. Rev.* 751, 751 (1986) (noting that the courts must decide cases free from popular pressure).

[20] Michel Foucault, Archaeology of Knowledge and Discourse of Language, trans. A.M. Sheridan Smith (1972) 38.

as we do, or to create and maintain an 'imagined community...'"[21] The Court substantially contributes to the imagined community of the United States via interpretation of the peoples through the People. It provides a conceptual basis upon which to stabilize, order, and perpetuate its interpretation of the Constitution. In so doing, it effectively attenuates the complex and diverse actualities that affect and effect the character and content of the peoples as expressed in the fundamental law.

The Court's power of review and supremacy gives rise to ordered arrangements that classify and govern the modalities of subjects' existence—at times detrimental to segments of the population.[22] Review and supremacy bestow a legislative power onto the Court. This legislative power is highly problematic in a democratic political context because of the nature of the Court's power. "[T]his Court is not a legislature ... Under the Constitution, judges have power to say what the law is, not what it should be. The people who ratified the Constitution authorized

[21] Steven D. Smith, Law as Language? 63 *Mercer L. R.* 891, 895 (2012) (emphasis added), available https://digitalcommons.law.mercer.edu/jour_mlr/vol63/iss3/8.

[22] See, e.g., *Buck v. Bell*, 274 U.S. 200, 207 (1927) (wherein the Court found that a State law permitting compulsory sterilization of the unfit, including the intellectually disabled, "for the protection and health of the state" did not violate the Due Process clause of the Fourteenth Amendment. "We have seen more than once that the public welfare may call upon the best citizens for their lives. It would be strange if it could not call upon those who already sap the strength of the State for these lesser sacrifices, often not felt to be such by those concerned, to prevent our being swamped with incompetence. It is better for all the world, if instead of waiting to execute degenerate offspring for crime, or to let them starve for their imbecility, society can prevent those who are manifestly unfit from continuing their kind."). Id. See also Marvin L. Astrada, Death, Law & Politics: The Effects of Embracing a Liberty-Restrictive vs. a Liberty-Enhancing Interpretation of Habeas Corpus, 48 *U. BALTIMORE L. R.* 156 (2019), available https://scholarworks.law.ubalt.edu/ublr/vol48/iss2/2. "The debate that contextualizes modern habeas thus centers on the degree to which federal courts should provide substantive oversight over state capital punishment schema. Under a restrictive view, federal courts should apply a rational basis of review, rendering oversight minimal, and under an expansionist view, federal courts should apply strict scrutiny because 'Constitutional guarantees of habeas corpus and the fundamental rights of life and liberty can only be protected under a system of judicial review which is strict in capital cases . ...' These opposing positions reflect a fundamental tension in habeas between preserving the integrity of state power and ensuring that the law, in actuality, provides due process and representational fairness." Id.

courts to exercise neither force nor will but merely judgment."[23] Judgment, however, has become the means by which review and supremacy are embedded into the interpretive enterprise. In regard to classification, the Court has noted that,

> Classification is the most inveterate of our reasoning processes. We can scarcely think or speak without consciously or unconsciously exercising it. It must therefore obtain in and determine legislation; but it must regard real resemblances and real differences between things and persons, and class them in accordance with their pertinence to the purpose in hand. Classification like the one with which we are here dealing is said to be the development of the philosophic thought of the world and is opening the door to legalized experiment."[24]

It is the Court, however, that functions as the textual interpretive classifier, gatekeeper for what constitutes constitutionality. "To me the constitution appears, in every line of it, to be a contract, which, in legal language, may be denominated tripartite. The parties are the people, the states, and the United States. It is returning in a circle to contend, that it professes to be the exclusive act of the people, for what have the people done but to form this compact?"[25] The peoples can be and has been minimized vis-à-vis the States and the national government, with the Court functioning as the singular actor to parse out benefits and losses under the fundamental law. When assessing the respective positions of the parties to the constitutional contract, it is the Court that decides what exactly does it mean for 1., something to be "implicit in

[23] *Obergefell v. Hodges*, 576 U.S. 644, 686 (2015) (Roberts, C.J. dissenting) (citations omitted).

[24] *Truax v. Corrigan*, 257 U.S. 312, 337–38 (1921). See Baker v. Carr, 369 U.S. 186, 210, 211, 217 (1962). (wherein the Court, considering the relationship between the federal and state governments and separation of powers, declared that, "it is the relationship between the judiciary and the coordinate branches of the Federal Government, and not the federal judiciary's relationship to the States, which gives rise to the 'political question' ... non-justiciability of a political question is primarily a function of the separation of powers ... Deciding whether a matter has in any measure been committed by the Constitution to another branch of government, or whether the action of that branch exceeds whatever authority has been committed, is itself a delicate exercise in constitutional interpretation, and is a responsibility of this Court as ultimate interpreter of the Constitution").

[25] *Martin v. Hunter's Lessee*, 14 U.S. 304, 373 (1816).

the concept of ordered liberty,"[26] 2., what type of conduct "shocks the conscience,"[27] and 3., what exactly constitutes an "undue burden"[28] in assessing rights, responsibilities, privileges and immunities,[29] obligations, prohibitions, and permissible content in policy spaces. The foregoing exemplify the establishment of an authoritative constitutional taxonomy that is Court-based, Court-centric, and Court-managed. Jacques Derrida's notion of textuality illuminates the dynamics of the Court's power of classification: "Textuality being constituted by differences and by differences from differences, it is by its nature absolutely heterogeneous and is constantly composing with the forces that tend to annihilate it."[30] In other, words, the interpretive enterprise is based on the purely subjective nature of the Court's taxonomy.[31]

The notion that language is accurately reflective of reality, be it social, political, economic, etc., is part of a greater sociocultural and ideological

[26] *Palko v. State of Connecticut*, 302 U.S. 319, 325 (1937), overruled by *Benton v. Maryland*, 395 U.S. 784 (1969).

[27] *Rochin v. California*, 342 U.S. 165, 172 (1952).

[28] *Planned Parenthood of S.E. Pennsylvania v. Casey*, 505 U.S. 833, 876 (1992).

[29] See, e.g., *Slaughter-House Cases*, 83 U.S. 36, 78 (1873). (wherein the Court found that the protection of individuals from State government actions was not the purpose of the Privileges or Immunities Clause, that the Clause was never meant to be a basis on which courts could strike down State law. The Court noted that, "such a construction [of the Privileges or Immunities Clause] followed by the reversal of the judgments of the Supreme Court of Louisiana in these cases, would constitute this court a perpetual censor upon all legislation of the States, on the civil rights of their own citizens, with authority to nullify such as it did not approve as consistent with those rights, as they existed at the time of the adoption of this amendment. ... We are convinced that no such results were intended by the Congress which proposed these amendments, nor by the legislatures of the States which ratified them.") Id. See also Laurence H. Tribe Taking Text and Structure Seriously: Reflections on Free-Form Method in Constitutional Interpretation, 108 *Harvard L. R.* 1221 (1995).

[30] Jacques Derrida, "Dissemination: From Plato's Pharmacy" 1830–1876, 1849, trans. Barbara Johnson in The Norton Anthology of Theory & Criticism, ed. Vincent B. Leitch, et al., 2001.

[31] Alexander Bickel notes that, "Democracy ... means that a representative majority has the power to accomplish a reversal ... [When the Court strikes down legislation,] it thwarts the will of representatives of the actual people of the here and now ... That, without mystic overtones, is what actually happens," quoted in Jed Rubenfeld, Reading the Constitution As Spoken, 104 *Yale L.J.* 1119, 1133 (1995).

enterprise.[32] "[I]t is one thing to say: This is my opinion, and another to say: This is true."[33] The Court directly shapes society by the nature of its classification rooted in elitism and a closed process accessible only to the Court's personnel as far as which cases merit a hearing, discussion, argumentation, and interpretation. The Court's interpretation of the fundamental law via review and supremacy is "pervasive in its personal, political, economic, aesthetic, psychological, moral, ethical, and social consequences that they leave no part of [the people] untouched, unaffected unaltered."[34] Consider, for example, the case of a right to die via assisted suicide, in which the Court stated that,

> this Court's decisions lead to the conclusion that respondents' asserted "right" to assistance in committing suicide is not a fundamental liberty interest protected by the Due Process Clause. The Court's established method of substantive-due-process analysis has two primary features: First,

[32] In the Federalist no. 37, James Madison's perspicacious analysis of language undermines the Court enterprise of attempting to definitively or clearly fix constitutional meaning in space and time (until the ken of the Court is augmented by future members of the Brethren: "All new laws, though penned with the greatest technical skill, and passed on the fullest and most mature deliberation, are considered as more or less obscure and equivocal, until their meaning be liquidated and ascertained by a series of particular discussions and adjudications. Besides the obscurity arising from the complexity of objects, and the imperfection of the human faculties, the medium through which the conceptions of men are conveyed to each other adds a fresh embarrassment. The use of words is to express ideas. Perspicuity, therefore, requires not only that the ideas should be distinctly formed, but that they should be expressed by words distinctly and exclusively appropriate to them. But no language is so copious as to supply words and phrases for every complex idea, or so correct as not to include many equivocally denoting different ideas. Hence it must happen that however accurately objects may be discriminated in themselves, and however accurately the discrimination may be considered, the definition of them may be rendered inaccurate by the inaccuracy of the terms in which it is delivered. And this unavoidable inaccuracy must be greater or less, according to the complexity and novelty of the objects defined. When the Almighty himself condescends to address mankind in their own language, his meaning, luminous as it must be, is rendered dim and doubtful by the cloudy medium through which it is communicated. Here, then, are three sources of vague and incorrect definitions: indistinctness of the object, imperfection of the organ of conception, inadequateness of the vehicle of ideas. Any one of these must produce a certain degree of obscurity." The Federalist, no. 37 (James Madison), available https://avalon.law.yale.edu/18th_century/fed37.asp.

[33] Jean Francois Lyotard and Jean-Loup Thebaud, Just Gaming , trans. Wlad Godzich (1999) 57.

[34] Marshall McLuhan and Quentin Fiore, The Medium is the Massage: An Inventory of Effects (1967) 8, 26.

> the Court has regularly observed that the Clause specially protects those fundamental rights and liberties which are, objectively, deeply rooted in this Nation's history and tradition. Second, the Court has required a "careful description" of the asserted fundamental liberty interest.[35]

Whether one agrees with the right asserted, it is the Court's personnel that will decide, based on its interpretation of history, what the constitutional stature of a claimed right will be via the People.

The Court's constitutional discourse, premised on converting the peoples into the People through its classificatory power, is "an important vector of power. What matters is to control the production and meaning of information in a given context ... Control of information is necessary in order to influence future developments."[36] Court opinions are informational events that proclaim what constitutes the fabric of the fundamental law which governs the polity, as well as what constitutes the peoples under the fundamental law. This can have—and has had—deleterious consequences for the peoples when the Court's notions of the People negatively impacts the peoples.[37] Court opinions are constitutive of knowledge. Knowledge of the Constitution's meaning, purpose, continuity, change, and trajectory, in the form of Court opinions, has profound consequences for the peoples. "Our idea of what belongs to the realm of reality is given for us in the [epistemic] concepts which we use."[38]

In the case of the People as an exercise of classification, the Court has, at various stages in history, maintained its position of their being a

[35] *Washington v. Glucksberg*, 521 U.S. 702, 702–3 (1997).

[36] Paul Patton, intro., The Gulf War Did Not Take Place by Jean Baudrillard, trans. Paul Patton (1991) 12–13.

[37] See, e.g., *Korematsu v. United States*, 323 U.S. 214 (1944) (upholding the exclusion of Japanese Americans from the West Coast Military Area during World War II.); *Bowers v. Hardwick*, 478 U.S. 186 (1986) (upholding constitutionality of a Georgia sodomy law criminalizing oral and anal sex in private between consenting adults); *Lone Wolf v. Hitchcock*, 187 U.S. 553 (1903) (finding that the "plenary power" of Congress gave it authority to abrogate treaty obligations between U.S. and Native American tribes unilaterally); *Cumming v. Richmond County Board of Education*, 175 U.S. 528 (1899) (sanctioning de jure segregation of races in American schools.); and *Ozawa v. United States*, 260 U.S. 178 (1922) (term "white person" was meant to indicate only a person of the Caucasian race, so Japanese were not "free white persons" within the meaning of the law.).

[38] Martin Hollis and Steve Smith, Explaining and Understanding International Relations 83 (1990).

People—as opposed to a peoples-based legal process informed by variegated economic, political, and sociocultural variables. Justice Harlan, for instance, dissenting in *Plessy*, was quite certain that,

> in view of the Constitution, in the eye of the law, there is in this country no superior, dominant, ruling class of citizens. There is no caste here. Our Constitution is color-blind, and neither knows nor tolerates classes among citizens. In respect of civil rights, all citizens are equal before the law. The humblest is the peer of the most powerful. The law regards man as man, and takes no account of his surroundings or of his color when his civil rights as guaranteed by the supreme law of the land are involved. It is, therefore, to be regretted that this high tribunal, the final expositor of the fundamental law of the land, has reached the conclusion that it is competent for a State to regulate the enjoyment by citizens of their civil rights solely upon the basis of race.[39]

The People, despite its being incongruent with the empirical actualities of the peoples that reside within the jurisdiction of the fundamental law as interpreted by the Court, e.g., the vast unequal distribution of wealth, mass incarceration, massive disparities in health care, housing, and employment opportunities based on class sector, as well as racial and ethnic considerations,[40] remains a pillar of the Court's power.

The People functions as a conceptual instrumentation to definitively classify, reify, and perpetuate the primary values of effective, efficient, and vigorous government through Union by attenuating and curbing the peoples themselves expressed in the legislatures of their respective States.[41] "Not only were the senate and presidency intended to check the

[39] *Plessy v. Ferguson*, 163 U.S. 537, 559 (1896).

[40] See, e.g., Angela Hanks, Danyelle Solomon, and Christian E. Weller, Systematic Inequality: How America's Structural Racism Helped Create the Black-White Wealth Gap, Center For American Progress, February 21, 2018, available https://www.americanprogress.org/issues/race/reports/2018/02/21/447051/systematic-inequality/; Rakesh Kochhar & Anthony Cilluffo, Key Findings on the Rise in Income Inequality Within America's Racial & Ethnic Groups, Pew Research Center, July 12, 2018, available https://www.pewresearch.org/fact-tank/2018/07/12/key-findings-on-the-rise-in-income-inequality-within-americas-racial-and-ethnic-groups/.

[41] See *Texas v. White*, 74 U.S. 700, 720 (1868), *overruled in part by Morgan v. U.S.*, 113 U.S. 476 (1885) ("The word 'State' 'describes sometimes a people or community of individuals united more or less closely in political relations, inhabiting temporarily or permanently the same country; often it denotes only the country or territorial region

power of popular majorities, but so, too, it could be argued, was the judiciary ... the judiciary was given a charter by many Federalists to assume legislative functions. Hamilton wrote in Federalist 78 that 'it is far more rational for suppose that the courts were designed to be an intermediate body between the people and the legislature in order, among other things, to keep the latter within the limits assigned to their authority.'"[42] The Court, from a macroscopic perspective, has been consistent in asserting its power to check the peoples. Indeed, Justices of the Court have recognized the elitist and antidemocratic nature of Court power. For instance, the "subjective nature of Justice Stevens' standard [in McDonald] is also apparent from his claim that it is the courts' prerogative—indeed their *duty*—to update the Due Process Clause so that it encompasses new

inhabited by such a community; not unfrequently it is applied to the government under which the people live; at other times it represents the combined idea of people, territory, and government. It is not difficult to see, that, in all these senses, the primary conception is that of a people or community. The people, in whatever territory dwelling, either temporarily or permanently, and whether organized under a regular government or united by looser and less definite relations, constitute the State. ... *In the Constitution, the term 'State' most frequently expresses the combined idea just noticed, of people, territory, and government.* A State, in the ordinary sense of the Constitution, is a political community of free citizens, occupying a territory of defined boundaries, organized under a government sanctioned and limited by a written constitution, and established by the consent of the governed. But the term is also used to express the idea of a people or political community, as distinguished from the government ... *It is the union of such States under a common constitution which forms the distinct and greater political unit which that constitution designates as the United States, and makes of the people and States which compose it one people and one country.*'").

[42] Isaac Kramnick, Intro to "The Federalist Papers," by James Madison, Alexander Hamilton & John Jay (1987) 51.

freedoms the Framers were too narrow-minded to imagine."[43] As noted by Chief Justice Roberts in *Obergefell*,

> It can be tempting for judges to confuse our own preferences with the requirements of the law. But as this Court has been reminded throughout our history, the Constitution 'is made for people of fundamentally differing views.' Accordingly, 'courts are not concerned with the wisdom or policy of legislation.' The majority today neglects that restrained conception of the judicial role. It seizes for itself a question the Constitution leaves to the people, at a time when the people are engaged in a vibrant debate on that question. And it answers that question based not on neutral principles of constitutional law, but on its own 'understanding of what freedom is and must become.[44]

In light of the above, consider the Court's use of "facts" in constructing constitutional discourse. Facts "all contribute only to setting the problem, not to its solution... doubt can exist only where a question exists, a question only where an answer exists, and an answer only

[43] *McDonald v. City of Chicago, Ill.*, 561 U.S. 742, 793–95, 803 (2010) (Scalia, J. concurring) (citations omitted). Justice Scalia further notes that Justice Stevens proclaims that the Court "must 'do justice to [the Clause's] urgent call and its open texture' by exercising the 'interpretive discretion the latter embodies.' (Why the *people* are not up to the task of deciding what new rights to protect, even though it is *they* who are authorized to make changes, see U.S. Const., Art. V, is never explained.) And it would be 'judicial abdication' for a judge to 'tur[n] his back' on *his* task of determining what the Fourteenth Amendment covers by 'outsourc[ing]' the job to 'historical sentiment'—that is, by being guided by what the American people throughout our history have thought. It is only we judges, exercising our 'own reasoned judgment,' who can be entrusted with deciding the Due Process Clause's scope—which rights serve the Amendment's 'central values'—which basically means picking the rights we want to protect and discarding those we do not. Justice Stevens resists this description, insisting that his approach provides plenty of 'guideposts' and 'constraints' to keep courts from 'injecting excessive subjectivity' into the process. Plenty indeed—and that alone is a problem. The ability of omnidirectional guideposts to constrain is inversely proportional to their number. But even individually, each lodestar or limitation he lists either is incapable of restraining judicial whimsy or cannot be squared with the precedents he seeks to preserve ... The implication of Justice Stevens' call for abstention is that if We The Court conclude that They The People's answers to a problem are silly, we are free to 'interven[e],' but if we too are uncertain of the right answer, or merely think the States may be on to something, we can loosen the leash." *McDonald v. City of Chicago, Ill.*, 561 U.S. 742, 793–95, 803 (2010) (Scalia, J. concurring) (citations omitted).

[44] *Obergefell v. Hodges*, 576 U.S. 644, 687–88 (2015) (Roberts, C.J. dissenting) (citations omitted).

where something can be said."[45] Facts, while empirically based, assume different weights based on operative sociocultural and economic factors. For example, the Court has stated in the context of precedent that, irrespective of the facts, "in most matters it is more important that the applicable rule of law be settled than that it be settled right."[46] Furthermore, the Court is able to interpolate facts so that they are in/operative in a particular case or set of cases, or facts are distinguished to align with or deviate away from a particular interpretation. Compare, for instance, *Hepburn v. Griswold*[47] and the *Legal Tender Cases*,[48] wherein the Court overruled itself in two years time based, arguably, on a change of personnel on the Court.[49] The Court's reasoning that, "Because independent agencies wield substantial power with no accountability to either the President or the people, they 'pose a significant threat to individual liberty and to the constitutional system of separation of powers and checks and balances,'"[50] equally applies to the position, role, and exercise of Court power itself. The Court is an independent political and legal actor that is not accountable to the peoples. Rather, it is accountable to the People—a "factual" construct of its own design and implementation.

Power involves utilizing facts so as to inject "realness and referentiality everywhere, to convince us of the reality of the [political], of the gravity of

[45] Ludwig Wittgenstein, Tractatus Logico-Philosophicus, trans. D.F. Pears & B.F. McGuiness (1975). 88

[46] *Burnet v. Coronado Oil & Gas Co.*, 285 U.S. 393, 406 (1932), overruled in part by *Helvering v. Bankline Oil Co.*, 303 U.S. 362 (1938), and overruled in part by *Helvering v. Mountain Producers Corp.*, 303 U.S. 376 (1938). See also David R. Dow, When Law Bows to Politics: Explaining *Payne v. Tennessee*, 26 U.C. Davis L. Rev. 157 (1992–1993).

[47] 75 U.S. 603, 604 (1869) (finding that, when case arises for judicial determination and decision depends on alleged inconsistency of legislative provision with fundamental law, it is plain duty of Supreme Court to compare act with Constitution, and if act cannot on fair construction be reconciled with Constitution, to give effect to constitution rather than statute.), overruled in part by *Leg. Tender Cases,* 79 U.S. 457 (1870).

[48] 79 U.S. 457 (1870) (Finding that the legal tender acts would be declared unconstitutional if there was a clear incompatibility with the Constitution but such conclusion would not be reached unless incompatibility plainly appeared).

[49] See Joseph M. Cormack, The Legal Tender Cases—A Drama of American Legal and Financial History (1929). Faculty Publications. 1497, available https://scholarship.law.wm.edu/facpubs/1497; Charles Fairman, Mr. Justice Bradley's Appointment to the Supreme Court and the Legal Tender Cases, 54 *Harvard L. R.* 977 (1941).

[50] *Seila L. LLC v. Consumer Fin. Protec. Bureau*, 140 S. Ct. 2183, 2212 (2020).

the [political] economy and the finalities of production."[51] The interpretations proffered by the Court of the fundamental law are "treated as their own autonyms and set in motion in a way that is supposed to render them mutually engendering."[52] Take, for example, the dissent in *Casey:* "the joint opinion's argument is based solely on generalized assertions about the national psyche, on a belief that the people of this country have grown accustomed to the Roe decision over the last 19 years and have 'ordered their thinking and living around' it. As an initial matter, one might inquire how the joint opinion can view the 'central holding' of Roe as so deeply rooted in our constitutional culture, when it so casually uproots and disposes of that same decision's trimester framework."[53] The power to have subjects "order their thinking" around or rather on the Court's word, opinion, interpretation of the fundamental law, with no external referents other than the Court itself as the ultimate referent, produces a closed system of thought that privileges Court supremacy. In the case of the Peoples, its classificatory power enables the Court to proclaim that, "For all the great purposes for which the Federal government was formed, we are one people, with one common country,"[54] ablating the problematic historical as well as present actualities that characterize American politics and society.[55]

LAPP thus explicitly acknowledges the systemic role of ideology (and, by implication, policymaking) dimensions of the Court's power.[56] The

[51] Jean Baudrillard, Simulations, trans. Paul Foss, Philip Beitchman &Paul Patton (1983) 42.

[52] Jean F. Lyotard, The Postmodern Condition: A Report on Knowledge, trans. Geoff Bennington & Brian Massumi, fwd. Fredric Jameson (1984) 35.

[53] *Planned Parenthood of S.E. Pennsylvania v. Casey*, 505 U.S. 833, 957 (1992).

[54] *Smith v. Turner*, 48 U.S. 283, 492 (1849).

[55] See Katherine Schaeffer, 6 Facts About Economic Inequality in the U.S., Pew Research Center, February 7, 2020, available https://www.pewresearch.org/fact-tank/2020/02/07/6-facts-about-economic-inequality-in-the-u-s/.

[56] "When all of its seats are filled, the Supreme Court operates with either a conservative or liberal majority. As a result, on politically controversial issues, the Court majority is able to impose its preferences on the entire country. These one-sided decisions leave the losing side—often half or more of the public—without a voice in the shaping of constitutional policy. That half of the public lacks meaningful representation on the critical judicial decisions that define the extent of governmental power and the breadth of a person's constitutional rights … a Justice's political philosophy does matter." David

systemic properties of the Court's power manifest in the American judiciary as a whole, exerting influence and control over the entire federal and state judicial actors. LAPP's explanatory power stems from the fact that a "judicial system can be conceptualized as encompassing all interactions in a society involved in the authoritative allocation of values by the judicial authorities of specified courts. Values are allocated by court decisions, procedural rules and court orders."[57] The elitist component of the Court's place, role, and power in constitutional order and as the supreme and unaccountable judicial authority viewed through a MEF lens, in conjunction with LAPP perspective, highlights the fact that all "law is social. Every bit of law activity may, it is true, be stated as a sum of individual 'acts;' but every bit may also be stated in group terms."[58]

The diverse and complex dynamics of the peoples drop out when put forth as the People in the Court's discourse—whether in the form of a majority, plurality, concurring, and dissenting opinions.[59] "[N]o official [opinion] ever contains the whole truth. Events are dictated by number of mitigating circumstances and a whole system of values and customs that can never be conveyed in print."[60]

Orentlicher, Politics and the Supreme Court: The Need for Ideological Balance, 79 *U. Pitt. L. Rev.* 411, 412–14 (2018).

[57] Sheldon Goldman & Thomas P. Jahnige, Eastonian Systems Analysis and Legal Research, 2 *RUTGERS-CAM L.J.* 285, 288 (1970).

[58] Arthur F. Bentley, The Process of Government (1908) 277. See also David S. Law, How to Rig the Federal Courts, 99 *Geo. L. J.* 779, 785–87 (2011).

[59] "There is, first, no such thing as a uniquely determined common good that all people could agree on or be made to agree on by the force of rational argument. This is due not primarily to the fact that some people may want things other than the common good but to the much more fundamental fact that to different individuals and groups the common good is bound to mean different things. This fact, hidden from the utilitarian by the narrowness of his outlook on them world of human valuations, will introduce rifts on questions of principle which cannot be reconciled by rational argument because ultimate values—our conceptions of what life and what society should be—are beyond the range of mere logic. They may be bridged by compromise in some cases but not in others … [at times] facing irreducible differences of ultimate values which compromise could only maim and degrade." Joseph Schumpeter, Capitalism, Socialism, and Democracy, in THE DEMOCRACY SOURCEBOOK, eds. Robert Dahl, Ian Shapiro, & Jose Antonio Cheibub (2003) 6 (discussing of the complexities and tensions underpinning notions of a common will in a political community premised on democratic representation).

[60] Huey P. Newton, The Huey P. Newton Reader, ed. David Hilliard & Donald Weise (2002) 114.

That these interpretive permutations, in the form of Court opinions, are the only ones that ultimately matter in positing the meaning of the Constitution for society as a whole has weighty consequences for the character and content of the polity, and the democratic society the Court "serves." Through its pronouncements, the Court exercises the power to name, classify, and control public thought and perception through the law, and this has a direct impact on representational politics and rights thinking.[61] That the Court's pronouncements can only be overturned by constitutional amendment or the Court itself serves to highlight the importance of critically appraising the People. Concepts and words "are bearers and generators of ideas ... not only do they transmit ... ideas and things ... language thinks, thinks us and thinks for us at least as much as we think through it."[62] The dissent in *Obergefell*, irrespective of whether the holding is "correct" or "incorrect," notes the consequence of the Court's construction, interpretation of the peoples via the People:

> Today's decree says that my Ruler, and the Ruler of 320 million Americans coast-to-coast, is a majority of the nine lawyers on the Supreme Court. The opinion in these cases is the furthest extension in fact—and the furthest extension one can even imagine—of the Court's claimed power to create 'liberties' that the Constitution and its Amendments neglect to mention. This practice of constitutional revision by an unelected committee of nine,

[61] See, e.g., *United States v. Martinez-Fuerte*, 428 U.S. 543, 543 (1976) (wherein the Court found that Government or public interest in having the U.S. border patrol set up internal checkpoints up to 100 air miles within the interior of the U.S. "outweighs the constitutionally protected interest of the private citizen."). *Martinez-Fuerte* "is a prime example of how a country can incrementally lose its rights despite retaining them on paper. The Fourth Amendment was conceived to protect against unreasonable search and seizures. In other words, if the government wants to invade someone's privacy, they had better get a warrant or have probable cause (which entails having an articulable reason and more than a "hunch"). Currently, the U.S. border patrol employs a dragnet method of inspection where every vehicle passing through is questioned. This makes suspicionless stops the modus operandi of these checkpoints. As such, this practice blatantly goes against the spirit of the amendment and effectively sends the message that rights can be disregarded if it is inconvenient to honor them. If repealing the Fourth Amendment was proposed in Congress tomorrow, America would have a revolution by lunch. But if the Fourth Amendment is slowly chipped away over the years as it has been, no one protests and fewer notice." Apurva Shrestha, "Repeal *United States v. Martinez-Fuerte*," The Breeze, Jan 13, 2019, available https://www.breezejmu.org/opinion/opinion-repeal-united-states-v-martinez-fuerte/article_14e6d038-1759-11e9-a248-af26d49efe23.html.

[62] Jean Baudrillard, Passwords, trans. Chris Turner (2003) xiii.

> always accompanied (as it is today) by extravagant praise of liberty, robs the People of the most important liberty they asserted in the Declaration of Independence and won in the Revolution of 1776: the freedom to govern themselves.[63]

The Court's self-prescribed status as final arbiter of the Constitution's meaning is based on the "existence of a language whose rules of functioning cannot themselves be demonstrated but are the object of a consensus."[64] The consensus in constitutional discourse is structured by the Court via the People. The peoples are converted into an object of knowledge via the People that the Court is empowered to "find" in the Constitution. Short of constitutional amendment, Court pronouncements have no external authority to answer to, thereby providing no viable alternative terms by which to conceptualize and (re)configure constitutional reality. The dissent's reasoning in *Casey* notes that, a

> difficulty ... lies in [the Court's] assumption that cases that are 'intensely divisive' can be readily distinguished from those that are not. The question of whether a particular issue is 'intensely divisive' enough to qualify for special protection is entirely subjective and dependent on the individual assumptions of the Members of this Court. In addition, because the Court's duty is to ignore public opinion and criticism on issues that come before it, its Members are in perhaps the worst position to judge whether a decision divides the Nation deeply enough to justify such uncommon protection.[65]

This assumption underpins how the political and legal context and process is regulated and circumscribed, wherein the Court articulates the authoritative or legitimate standards by which "facts" are conceptualized, applied, and adjudged. Language, discourse, the written and spoken word—each is intrinsically malleable, each is a site of political contestation by elites over what is actual and possible in thought and practice, and what exactly constitutes (constitutional) reality.[66]

[63] *Obergefell v. Hodges*, 576 U.S. 644, 713–14 (2015) (Roberts, C.J. dissenting).

[64] Lyotard, "Postmodern," supra note 52 at 43.

[65] *Planned Parenthood of S.E. Pennsylvania v. Casey*, 505 U.S. 833, 958–59 (1992).

[66] See *Pacific Gas & Electric v. G.W. Thomas Drayage & Rigging Co.*, 442 P.2d 641 (Cal. 1968): If words had absolute and constant references, it might be possible to

Law and its interpretation in the form of Court opinions are thus part of a complex and systemic government activity and context. "Each particular law rests in a great habit background of law, that is, has its place in the system. The value of each law, its meaning, is known only in terms of the values and meanings of the other activities which taken all together make up the system."[67] The impact of the elitist, nondemocratic and nonrepresentational character of the Court has on democratic government, society, and the overarching constitutional order is thus brought to the fore.

In contestations over the "correct" meaning, truth, of a particular state of affairs, there is a potential to regard language as an objective naming process, wherein words simply correspond to that which is named. Such a conceptualization of discourse "assumes that ready-made ideas exist before words... [this] lets us assume that the linking of a name and a thing is a very simple operation."[68] Take, for example, the Court's sociocultural, political, and legal characterization of aliens and the annexation of foreign peoples via territories into the U.S. political unit. "If those possessions are inhabited by alien races, differing from us in religion, customs, laws, methods of taxation, and modes of thought, the administration of government and justice, according to Anglo-Saxon principles, may for a time be impossible; and the question at once arises whether large concessions ought not to be made for a time, that ultimately our own theories may be carried out, and the blessings of a free government under the Constitution extended to them."[69]

Rather than argue for the primacy or intrinsic correctness of a particular interpretation, as the Court does in its constitutional discourse, it may be more conducive to enhancing representative government to focus on the fact that discourse and signifiers have a multiplicity of meaning

discover ... intention in the words themselves and in the manner in which they were arranged. Words, however, do not have absolute and constant referents. .... The meaning of particular words or groups of words varies with the . . . verbal context and surrounding circumstances and purposes in view of the linguistic education and experience of their users and their hearers or readers (not excluding judges). ... A word has no meaning apart from these factors; much less does it have an objective meaning, one true meaning." Id. at 644–45 (quoting Arthur L. Corbin, The Interpretation of Words and the Parol Evidence Rule, 50 *CORNELL L.Q.* 161, 187 [1965]).

67 Bentley, supra note 58 at 284.

68 Ferdinand De Saussure, "Course in General Linguistics," in The Norton Anthology of Theory & Criticism, eds. Vincent B. Leitch, et al. (2018) 826.

69 *Downes v. Bidwell*, 182 U.S. 244, 286–87 (1901).

and truths immanent within them. This opens up the space of permissible thought when analyzing the Court's power, its pronouncements on the fundamental law, the People, and the power dynamics, assumptions, and consequentialness of Court opinions. If the people truly have a substantive voice, presence, in government and governance, then divesting the Court of its singular monopoly on words, meaning, history—in short, conditional discourse, may have a salubrious effect in bringing this about.

The Court's closed constitutional discourse, premised on review and supremacy, through singular classification of what does and does not merit constitutional protection and why or why not, empowers it to "declare [identity], deny ambiguities, and proclaim univocal conclusions."[70] The power to speak before all others infuses the Court's People with truth-value that may or may not reflect the actual people. Truth can subjugate as well as "enlighten" humankind. The question then becomes, when assessing the Court's power through MEF and LAPP, how does the Court's position and power in the overarching system of government and governance translate into constitutional truth, knowledge, and public policy in a representative democratic system.

The elite group interest that underpins constitutional interpretation is important to analyze, especially in the context of a democratic political system in which representation entails control of government by the people (rather than the People) of the United States. The elite group interest that underpins the constitutional jurisprudence of the Court reflects what may be considered norms, values, and ideological interests that are at odds with notions of genuine representative government. "What we have then is not a series of laws ... law activities, disconnected from one another like so many pebbles in a pile, to use a common illustration. Instead, we have these law activities so knit together in larger groups that by analysis on a different plane we can point out what we may call

[70] Stephen M. Feldman, The Supreme Court in a Postmodern World: A Flying Elephant, 84 *Minn. L. Rev.* 673 (2000). "[C]ultural traditions cannot themselves be a normative basis for conflict resolution in advanced societies: consensus can only be discursively achieved through argumentation in dis-course; it is not already contained in a concrete form of life. Nor can it be reduced to a model of praxis which fails to distinguish between ethics and politics. Discursive consensus is therefore to be contrasted to notions of cultural consensus and civic praxis." Gerard Delanty, Habermas and Occidental Rationalism: The Politics of Identity, Social Learning, and the Cultural Limits of Moral Universalism, Sociological Theory, vol. 15, no. 1 (March, 1997) 33.

a single group activity representing a whole set of laws."[71] The fundamental law thus becomes a vehicle for promoting government over "an imagined political community ... It is imagined because the members of even the smallest nation will never know most of their fellow-members, meet them, or even hear of them, yet in the minds of each lives the image of their communion ... In fact, all communities larger than primordial villages of face-to-face contact ... are imagined. Communities are to be distinguished by the style in which they are imagined."[72] The "style" of the law-givers as well as interpreters—each is imbricated with the other—is one that may not necessarily enhance representation of the people in the fullest sense of the term, nor may it facilitate accountability. How exactly is a life-tenured, antidemocratic, institution comprised of a discrete and insular sociocultural hyper-minority that is independent of those it ostensibly serves, to reflect the people qua people and not as a proxy through which elite rule is justified under the aegis of democracy? The elite interests and actors that populate and animate the machinery of government have "finite, if elastic, boundaries ... regardless of the actual inequality and exploitation that may prevail."[73]

[71] Bentley, supra note 58 at 285–6.

[72] Benedict Anderson, Imagined Communities: Reflections on the Origins and Spread of Nationalism 2nd ed. (1991) 5.

[73] Id. at 6.

CHAPTER 5

Step 5: Concluding Thoughts: Truth, the People, Court Power and Representative Politics

Abstract Law, as an ordering mechanism, as a repository for a polity's identity, and as a medium for the expression of societal sociocultural norms, values, and judgments, is a product and producer of a subject's being in the world. The actual, potential, and possible stem from the law as far as ordering a society. The character and content of a people can be located in the law, and how the law informs and transects the social, political, and economic dimensions of a society. By viewing the Court's power through the lens of a Mass/Elite framework and a Law as Process Perspective, we can begin the process of disaggregating the Court's power and assessing the impact it has on the American democratic representative political system.

Keywords Law · Representation · Discourse · Democratic politics · Court power

In the early twentieth century, Chief Justice Hughes declared that, "We are under a Constitution, but the Constitution is what the judges say it is."[1] This sentiment is in line with the Court's decree that, "the basic

[1] Charles Evans Hughes, "Speech before the Chamber of Commerce, Elmira, New York (3 May 1907)" in Addresses and Papers of Charles Evans Hughes, Governor of

M. L. Astrada, *Law, Society & Politics*,
https://doi.org/10.1007/978-3-030-66714-6_5

principle that the federal judiciary is supreme in the exposition of the law of the Constitution" is "a permanent and indispensable feature of our constitutional system."[2] A primary mechanism by which the Court has been able to operationalize this principle of interpretation has been the People. The Court has stated that, "As men whose intentions require no concealment generally employ the words which most directly and aptly express the ideas they intend to convey, the enlightened patriots who framed our constitution, and the people who adopted it, must be understood to have employed words in their natural sense, and to have intended what they have said.'"[3] The People, as expressed by John Jay in Federalist no. 2, in the Preamble, and as subsequently interpreted the Court, has indeed been consistent. It remains the purview of the judicial elite as far as interpreting the fundamental law.

Law, as an ordering mechanism, as a repository for a polity's identity, and as a medium for the expression of societal sociocultural norms, values, and judgments, is a product and producer of a subject's being in the world. Court opinions, as expositions of the definitive meaning of the fundamental law, are a "form of power that applies itself to immediate everyday life [and categorization of] the individual, marks him by his own individuality, attaches him to his own identity, imposes a law of truth upon him that he must recognize and others have to recognize in him."[4] The actual, potential, and possible stem from the interpretation of the fundamental law as far as ordering a society. The character and content of peoples can be located in the law, and how the law informs and transects the social, political, and economic dimensions of a society. "No matter how you identify politically, where you work, live, or play, we are all participants in an ongoing democratic experiment, the one framed and set in motion by James Madison and his contemporaries 231 years

New York, 1906–1908 (1908) 139. See Charles Evans Hughes, Columbia University Profile, available http://c250.columbia.edu/c250_celebrates/remarkable_columbians/charles_hughes.html#:~:text=Charles%20Evans%20Hughes&text=%22We%20are%20under%20a%20Constitution,the%20judges%20say%20it%20is.%22&text=Known%20as%20a%20master%20of,for%20his%20brilliant%20legal%20mind.

[2] *Cooper v. Aaron*, 358 U.S. 1, 18 (1958).

[3] *Kidd v. Pearson*, 128 U.S. 1, 20 (1888).

[4] Michel Foucault, "The Subject and Power," in The Essential Foucault, ed. Paul Rainbow & Nikolas Rose (2003) 130.

ago."[5] By viewing the Court through the lens of MEF and LAPP, we can begin a process of disaggregating the Court's power and assessing the impact it has on the American democratic representative political system. This exercise is important because the law is the means by which policy is effectuated. As noted by the dissent in *Obergefell*, "The Court's accumulation of power does not occur in a vacuum. It comes at the expense of the people."[6]

The United States, as a political unit, nation-state, though comprised of dissimilar types of peoples, based on, e.g., race, ethnicity, socioeconomic class, and generation, is ostensibly "held together," in part, through a

> shared understanding that we are all subject to and governed by something we call 'the Constitution'... But ... the Constitution seems to be a fiction, and the name or term is a fertile source of equivocation ... that antique document does not itself govern us ... when people refer to the Constitution they mean very different things[, such as] ... the words of the document as those words were understood at the time of enactment ... the subjective intentions of the people who wrote and enacted those words ... something more sociological, evolving and elusive: the 'traditions and collective conscience of our people,' [(*Griswold v. Connecticut*, 381 U.S. 479, 493 (1965) (quoting *Snyder v. Massachusetts*, 291 U.S. 97, 105 (1934))] ... Or ... *the Constitution is whatever the United States Supreme Court says it is* ...[7]

When deferring to or embracing the latter state of affairs, the Court's power to speak before all others in a univocal, unitary voice has profound consequences for the character and content of democratic representational politics. The elitist and process-based nature of the People provides the Court with a monopoly over the capacity to authoritatively and

[5] Kat Imhoff, The Constitution at 231: What Does 'We the People' Really Mean? *The Hill*, September 22, 2018, available https://thehill.com/opinion/white-house/407884-the-constitution-at-231-what-does-we-the-people-really-mean.

[6] *Obergefell v. Hodges*, 576 U.S. 644, 709 (2015) (Roberts, C.J. dissenting).

[7] Steven D. Smith, Law as Language? 63 *Mercer L. R.* 891, 895 (2012) (emphasis added), available https://digitalcommons.law.mercer.edu/jour_mlr/vol63/iss3/8. See also Steven D. Smith, What Does Constitutional Interpretation Interpret? in Expounding The Constitution: Essays In Constitutional Theory, ed. Grant Huscroft (2008).

definitively classify its subject population through interpretation of the fundamental law.

The law, as Michel Foucault observes, is part of a biopolitics in which power is exercised in a manner that can be characterized as the "power of regulation" to regularize life, which "consists in making live… the right to intervene to make live … [and] eliminating … deficiencies."[8] MEF and LAPP help highlight the "regularization of life," as Michel Foucault terms it, under constitutional discourse in the context of biopower and politics, is one that excludes, reduces, and emplaces thought and being in binary oppositions within which complexity, diversity, and the morass of human beings are simplified in the name of a pragmatic politics, which in turn, serves a narrowly defined identity for the purposes of wielding power in politics and policy.[9] In light of the closed, elitist, and nondemocratic nature of the Court's power, complex notions of representation are attenuated under the Court's constitutional jurisprudence.

That the Court, as an insulated, nondemocratic actor, can control the behavior of the mass of its subjects through the fundamental law renders it an awe-inspiring institution—one that cuts against the grain of democratic representative politics in the true sense of the term. The Court has declared that, "We do not sit as a super-legislature to determine the wisdom, need, and propriety of laws that touch economic problems, business affairs, or social conditions."[10] Yet, the Court's exercise of power in declaring itself to be the ultimate interpreter of the fundamental law has had this effect. Its decisions, such as *Roe v. Wade*[11] and *Citizens United v. FCC*,[12] among a plethora of others, have indeed had a powerful legislative effect on law, politics, and society that can only be undone through constitutional amendment or Court revisionism. The Court has declared that, "The constitution of the United States was designed for

[8] Michel Foucault, Society Must Be Defended, in THE NORTON ANTHOLOGY OF THEORY AND CRITICISM, eds. Vincent B. Leitch et al., 3d ed. (2018) 1445.

[9] Michel Foucault, "SOCIETY MUST BE DEFENDED": LECTURES AT THE COLLÈGE DE FRANCE, 1975–1976, ed. Mauro Bertani & Alessandro Fontana, trans. David Macey (2003) 247–49.

[10] *Griswold v. Connecticut*, 381 U.S. 479, 482 (1965).

[11] 410 U.S. 113 (1973).

[12] 558 U.S. 310 (2010).

the common and equal benefit of all the people of the United States."[13] Yet, as the American polity has always been—and finds itself more and more—fragmented, disjointed, and polarized, it is productive to subject the Court to a critical analysis that seeks to flesh out how it contributes to the greater government and governance in the legal and political context.[14]

MEF and LAPP provide lenses to identify and examine how the economic, political, judicial, and sociocultural intersect in the fundamental law, complicating and problematizing the Court's assertion that the "constitution of the United States was ordained and established, not by the states in their sovereign capacities, but emphatically, as the preamble of the constitution declares, by 'the people of the United States.'"[15] Antidemocratic elitism, as manifested in the Court and as a basis of its power, has had an enduring and profound impact on the peoples, American politics, and democratic representative government that is in theory authorized and legitimized by the peoples. The People is

[13] *Martin v. Hunter's Lessee*, 14 U.S. 304, 348 (1816). For a selection of counter-examples, which "involved the shameful, disdainful treatment by the powerful of minorities and their rights," and in which "the court sided with the powerful, consigning the minority often to generations of abuse and/or denial of fundamental rights," and which "unbiased observers agree that the decisions adversely impacted millions for several and sometimes many generations" (M. Kelly Tillery, The 10 Worst Supreme Court Decisions, Philadelphia Bar Association, 2010, available https://www.philadelphiabar.org/WebObjects/PBAReadOnly.woa/Contents/WebServerResources/CMSResources/TPL_summer2010_worst.pdf), see *Dred Scott v. Sandford*, 60 U.S. 393 (1857) (African slaves are not citizens under the Constitution and have no standing to sue); *United States v. Cruikshank*, 92 U.S. 542 (1875) (Bill of Rights did not apply to private actors or to state governments despite the adoption of the Fourteenth Amendment. It reversed criminal convictions for the civil rights violations committed in aid of anti-reconstruction murder); *Pace v. Alabama*, 106 U.S. 583 (1883) (affirming that Alabama's anti miscegenation statute was constitutional); *Plessy v. Ferguson*, 163 U.S. 537 (1896) (confirming separate but equal as constitutional); and *Buck v. Bell*, 274 U.S. 200 (1927) (a state statute permitting compulsory sterilization of the unfit, including the intellectually disabled, "for the protection and health of the state" did not violate the Due Process clause of the Fourteenth Amendment). Id.

[14] It is important to note that inactivity is as consequential as activity: "seemingly indifferent activity is a real group activity, even though the abstracting of an interest, a value, a meaning, in terms of other groups, seems difficult. It is a law activity like any other; the difficulty is only in the use of words to make it seem positively worthwhile." Arthur F. Bentley, The Process of Government (1908) 293.

[15] *Martin v. Hunter's Lessee*, 14 U.S. 304, 324 (1816).

an exemplar of how the peoples assume a subordinate role in the constitutional interpretive enterprise. Gaetano Mosca posits that, "There can be no human organization without rankings and subordinations. Any sort of hierarchy necessarily requires that some should command and others obey."[16] The Mass/Elite binary captures this observation. Every configuration of order has a regime(s) of truth, i.e., discursive as well as material "mechanisms and instances which enable a subject to distinguish true/false statements, the means by which each is sanctioned; the techniques and procedures accorded value in the acquisition of truth; the status of those who are charged with saying what counts as true."[17]

Truth, in its purest sense, can actually be repressive in that it delimits the space of thought and possibility. The antidemocratic, nonrepresentative nature of the Court's truth-producing discourse converts the very complex sociocultural people into the legal construct of the People. As a branch of government, it appropriates truth so as to accord itself the privilege of inclusion and exclusion, of what is or is not (can or cannot be) the case. Law and justice come into being within this paradigm. It is "truth that makes the laws, that produces the ["true"] discourse which, at least partially, decides, transmits itself, extends upon the effects of power. In the end, we are judged, condemned, classified, determined in our undertakings, destined to a certain mode of living or dying, as a function of the true discourses."[18] The Court's power lies, in part, in appearing to contain high degrees of objective truth-value that, in turn, provides the basis for its authority. Truth produces correctness; truth enables the production of constitutional truth regimes.[19]

The Court is the arbiter of legal actuality under the Constitution, and it defines the limits of a subject's legal personhood. The Court's constitutional discourse, and the knowledge it manufactures and disseminates, becomes the singular objective referent for comprehending the who, what, why, and how—e.g., in the form of rights, protections, obligations, and responsibilities—of the Constitution in the mundane and extraordinary contexts that define legal reality. The Court perpetuates and

[16] Gaetano Mosca, The Ruling Class, Hannah D. Kahn trans. (1939) 397.

[17] Michel Foucault, Power/Knowledge: Selected Interviews & Other Writings 1972–1977, ed. & trans. Colin Gordon (1980) 131.

[18] Id. at 94.

[19] See Id. at 39.

disseminates an epistemic discourse that contributes to the creation and propagation of new objects of "knowledge and accumulates new bodies of information. Knowledge and power are integrated with one another... It is not possible for power to be exercised without knowledge, and it is impossible for knowledge not to engender power."[20] The institutionalization of knowledge/power, in the guise of authoritative, objective discourse, systemically privileges particular enunciations of what is right over others. The Court reflects a rationalized administration of knowledge—an "administration of knowledge, a politics of knowledge, relations of power which pass via knowledge,"[21] power and truth. In the manufacture of power-precepts, it is important to keep in mind what type(s) of knowledge does an institution that wields "legitimate" authority seek to disqualify?

The production of truth is essential to the manufacture and deployment of power, influence, and control. Truth, therefore, an elusive, malleable, synthetic state of affairs is not independent of power, knowledge, or right. Indeed, truth's effect on the unthinking, uncritical subject leads to what Friedrich Nietzsche refers to as humankind's most false illusion, i.e., "a thing exists, therefore it is legitimate. Here one is concluding functionality from viability, and legitimacy from functionality."[22] The manufacture of truth rests with the actors/institutions that produce it, within the discourse that articulates and legitimizes a particular truth. "Truth is a political production as for political power; it is the object, under diverse forms, of immense diffusion and consumption; ... it is produced and transmitted under the control, dominant if not exclusive, of a few great political and economic apparatuses."[23] Being engaged in ascertaining and determining mass social consensus is part of the truth-enterprise. The People is thus a discursive construct invested with knowledge, truth, and power. The People reflects an ordering mechanism that is, in thought and practice, contrary to the fundamental political

[20] Id. at 51–52.

[21] Id. at 69.

[22] Fredrich Nietzsche, Human, All Too Human: A Book for Free Spirits, 2nd ed., R. J. Hollingdale, trans. (1996) 37.

[23] Foucault, "Power/Knowledge," supra note 17 at 132.

truths that are constitutive of American political culture, i.e., representative democratic politics. One should not, therefore, lose sight of the people in the Court's propagation of its constitutional discourse.

The Court has emphatically stated that,

> The constitution unavoidably deals in general language. It did not suit the purposes of the people, in framing this great charter of our liberties, to provide for minute specifications of its powers, or to declare the means by which those powers should be carried into execution. It was foreseen that this would be a perilous and difficult, if not an impracticable, task. The instrument was not intended to provide merely for the exigencies of a few years, but was to endure through a long lapse of ages, the events of which were locked up in the inscrutable purposes of Providence. It could not be foreseen what new changes and modifications of power might be indispensable to effectuate the general objects of the charter; and restrictions and specifications, which, at the present, might seem salutary, might, in the end, prove the overthrow of the system itself. Hence its powers are expressed in general terms ... to mould [sic] and model the exercise of its powers, *as its own wisdom*, and the public interests, should require.[24]

If this is the case, then the People, in light of MEF and LAPP, in thought and practice, is an artifice, a political formula.[25] The People, as an elite construct, that is an instrumental, pragmatic, reductionist, and control mechanism, privileges order, stability, and security via protection of the

[24] *Martin v. Hunter's Lessee*, 14 U.S. 304, 326–27 (1816) (emphasis added).

[25] See Mosca, supra note 16 at xv, xxxviii: "This legal and moral basis, or principle, on which the power of tie political class rests, is ... the 'political formula.' (Writers on the philosophy of law generally call it the 'principle of sovereignty.'" Id. at 70. Kahn, in her introduction to the text, expounds upon this concept, noting that Mosca "went on to develop his theory of the 'political formula.' There is always a ruling minority, but such minorities never stop at the brute fact of holding power. They justify their rule by theories or principles which are in turn based on beliefs or ethical systems which are accepted by those who are ruled. These 'political formulas' contain very little that could be described as "truth," but they should not be regarded as deliberate deceptions or mystifications on the part of scheming rulers. They express, rather, a deep need in human nature whereby the human being more readily defers to abstract universal principles than to the will of individual human beings ... Mosca sees that political formulas are invalid as "truth" but yet somehow determine the exterior aspects, at least, of whole civilizations, of social types that are immensely populous."

(elite) minority from the (mass) majority,[26] by way of bolstering Constitutional order over the independent interests of the peoples whom it supposedly serves, which in word (as opposed to deed) are to include non-elitist interpretations and articulations of Justice, Equality, Rule of Law, Substantive and Procedural Due Process, Fairness, and Equity. "Such is the language of the article creating and defining the judicial power of the United States. It is the voice of the whole American people solemnly declared, in establishing one great department of that government which was, in many respects, national, and in all, supreme."[27] The peoples get lost in translation. Part of this loss involves the notion that the People cuts against the grain of the democratic representative spirit of the law. Genuine representation encompasses the proposition that the law should not be "tainted by considerations of class or caste," and that "fairness of governmental processes, of due process" should animate the legal process.[28]

The People thus effectively operationalizes the invention of a homogenous population with equal or similar motives, interests, issues, ideological and political predispositions, cultural norms and values, and what exactly constitutes conditions and problems in the realms of law, politics, and society. "Our experience of another person ... no matter how close he

[26] See "Term of the Senate [26 June] 1787," Founders Online, National Archives, [Original source: The Papers of James Madison, vol. 10, 27 May 1787–3 March 1788, ed. Robert A. Rutland, Charles F. Hobson, William M. E. Rachal, and Frederika J. Teute. Chicago: The University of Chicago Press, 1977, 76–78.], available https://founders.archives.gov/documents/Madison/01-10-02-0044. "The man who is possessed of wealth, who lolls on his sofa or rolls in his carriage, cannot judge of the wants or feelings of the day laborer. The government we mean to erect is intended to last for ages. The landed interest, at present, is prevalent; but in process of time, when we approximate to the states and kingdoms of Europe; when the number of landholders shall be comparatively small, through the various means of trade and manufactures, will not the landed interest be overbalanced in future elections, and unless wisely provided against, what will become of your government? In England, at this day, if elections were open to all classes of people, the property of the landed proprietors would be insecure. An agrarian law would soon take place. If these observations be just, our government ought to secure the permanent interests of the country against innovation. Landholders ought to have a share in the government, to support these invaluable interests and to balance and check the other. They ought to be so constituted as to protect the minority of the opulent against the majority ... (Farrand, Records, I, 430–31)." Id.

[27] *Martin v. Hunter's Lessee*, 14 U.S. 304, 328 (1816).

[28] Mark G. Yudof, Equal Protection, Class Legislation & Sex Discrimination: One Small Cheer for Mr. Herbert Spencer's '"Social Statics," 88 *Mich. L. Rev.* 1366 (1990).

stands to us, can never be complete, so that we would have a logical right to a total evaluation of him; all evaluations are premature and are bound to be."[29] For this reason, it is incumbent upon the peoples to critically engage and appraise how conducive the People is positing and facilitating the general welfare and public interest for all of the subject population.

[29] Nietzsche supra note 22 at 28.

Index

M. L. Astrada, *Law, Society & Politics*,
https://doi.org/10.1007/978-3-030-66714-6

The manufacturer's authorised representative in the EU is Springer Nature Customer Service Centre GmbH, Europaplatz 3, 69115 Heidelberg, Germany. If you have any concerns regarding our products, please contact ProductSafety@springernature.com

Printed and bound by CPI Group (UK) Ltd, Croydon, CR0 4YY
30/09/2026
02225466-0007